WOMEN IN
POLITICS

WOMEN
★ IN ★
POLITICS

SHARON WHITNEY AND TOM RAYNOR

Franklin Watts / 1986
New York / London / Toronto / Sydney

Photographs courtesy of:
National Women's Political Caucus: pp. 13, 129;
UPI/Bettmann Newsphotos: pp. 27, 42, 47, 58, 101, 104, 114;
Sharon Whitney: pp. 87, 90.

Library of Congress Cataloging-in-Publication Data

Whitney, Sharon.
Women in politics.

Includes index.
Summary: Traces the history of women's involvement in
American politics, with profiles of women candidates,
mayors, governors, congressional representatives, and
cabinet members.
 1. Women in politics—United States—Juvenile
literature. 2. Politicians—United States—Biography—
Juvenile literature. [1. Women in politics.
 2. Politicians] I. Raynor, Thomas P. II. Title.
HQ1236.5.U6W48 1986 320'.088042 [920] 86-11149
ISBN 0-531-10243-2

CONTENTS

WOMEN IN POLITICS

★ 1 ★

WHAT MAKES JANE RUN?

When women won the vote in 1920 they didn't storm the gates rushing into politics as one might have supposed. Instead, women who were politically active—most of them suffragists who had worked for decades to get the Nineteenth Amendment—breathed a great sigh of relief and reckoned their work was done. Few saw themselves as candidates for office. In fact, women were scarcely heard from until almost fifty years later.

It was in the late 1960s and early 1970s that women started to become deeply involved in politics. The country was in a crisis. Ruinous treatment of the environment, an undeclared war in Vietnam, and state policies allowing racial discrimination angered many Americans. In small towns and big cities people were talking about the issues and channeling passionate beliefs into political action. Everywhere groups of people pulled together to march, to protest, and to get behind candidates who supported their ideas. Politics was hot, messy, but very accessible.

In this atmosphere, where questions of right and wrong were debated daily, women began to find a voice. Many learned that politics was not for men only. Women could articulate the problems and solutions as well as men. They had equal zest for taking action. They could forge a political philosophy and a vision of a better future.

Having awakened to the challenge of politics, many of these women then took the skills they learned working on men's campaigns and started to seek political power on their own. Where there had been only a handful of female candidates, increasing numbers now sought office as school board members, county commissioners, mayors, city councillors, state senators and representatives, and members of Congress.

In fifteen years the number of women in state legislatures, alone, tripled. And by the early 1980s, women's need to see other women at the top swelled to the point of insistence. Feminist groups vigorously lobbied the Democratic party to choose a woman as a vice presidential candidate. In 1984 they achieved this historic breakthrough at the Democratic National Convention.

> Being on the convention floor the evening Ferraro was nominated was the most exciting thing that has ever happened to me in my life, surpassed only by the birth of my son. We reporters tried, and mostly failed, to look objective. What was the point of pretending? We too had had to fight to be taken seriously, to get onto that floor. Ann Richards, the Texas state treasurer, and I hugged and cried. Dagmar Celeste, Ohio's first lady, danced and laughed. We felt proud of being women, standing tall as though everything had changed, as though from now on we would have a say in the future of the country.
>
> Jane O'Reilly
> Vogue magazine

The importance of a woman running for vice president of the United States could not be overrated. Women were now in major league politics.

"It's like the four-minute mile: the barriers are broken," said Robert Strauss, former Democratic national chair. In the course of the 1984 campaign, Geraldine Ferraro proved that women could take the heat in the biggest and roughest political contest. From now on fewer voters would be asking, "Should a woman run for high office?" More would be wondering, "Who will she be?"

PERSONALITY, SKILLS,
AND INTERESTS

The woman who runs for office at any level must first of all have abundant energy and patience. In the course of her campaign she'll have to talk to all kinds of people, from the PTA to the chamber of commerce. She'll speak to audiences, both friendly and aloof, and she'll probably go on radio and television to defend her views. If she's elected, these demands will continue with the added feature that the public now believes she "owes them" all her time and energy. Therefore, good communication skills are necessary to succeed in politics, along with a host of other skills.

Fran Ulmer, who headed a national organization of women mayors while serving as mayor of Juneau, Alaska, says that women who run cities share no obvious single trait or style. But like male mayors, they tend to be "articulate, personable and self-confident." These qualities emerge from a variety of backgrounds.

Ulmer surveyed thirty women mayors and found that nursing, education, and social work were the most common professions represented. There were also businesswomen, accountants, and homemakers who had spent years as civic volunteers. Dianne Feinstein of San Francisco went from college into public life serving on various boards and committees while being elected to progressively higher levels of office. Peggy Mensinger of Modesto, California, worked for twenty years as a community volunteer until her children were grown and she felt free to run for office.

But whatever her background, the successful politician needs to know strategies for getting support, according to Irene Natividad, president of the National Women's Political Caucus (NWPC). She has to be able to work in coalitions. This means being willing to trade support and to cooperate with politicians whose ideas may be different from her own.

The female politician must also be able to absorb the ups and downs of the legislative process and to rebound when she doesn't win. "It helps to know how to lose, how to give in," says Natividad. Early training in team sports rather than too much focus on individual achievement helps in learning how to roll with the punches, she says.

Natividad also believes that women have an initial advantage in running for office, which can help them if other factors are positive. "They are perceived as more compassionate, as innovative and interesting, and as a source of new ideas." This personality bonus can make a difference at the ballot box.

The successful politician must also be able to forget herself and learn what's important to the voters, according to Linda Hallenborg, a Georgia political activist and former vice president of NWPC. "It takes a person who can step outside herself and get the larger picture," she says. "She has to be able to get the lay of the land, be in sync with local culture."

Hallenborg, who moved to Atlanta from Pennsylvania, says it takes a special kind of perception to know what people want. When she entered politics in Georgia, she was keenly aware of the differences in personal style between persons in the Northeast and those in the South. "You have to have a feel for people—what is acceptable and nonthreatening to them." And because the politician is constantly on view, her responses must be genuine.

In politics, it helps very much to like people. Because political life can be one long series of meetings, liking people can be crucial. Overcoming differences, forging agreements, planning mutual goals—all depend on interaction. A woman running for office is wise to ask herself not only whether she will be accepted by the people, but whether she is open to others, too.

WHAT MAKES
JANE RUN?

Women in politics agree that a female candidate has to meet or exceed the qualifications of a male candidate. She also has to be prepared to deal with special problems unique to women in office. Ulmer says that "being a woman mayor brings out many similar stories: the sexist bias of some city departments like public works and police; the incredible loss of privacy (the celebrity phenomenon); and the difficult balance of family/

Representative Patricia Schroeder (D-Co.) addressed
a recent meeting of the National Women's Political
Caucus (NWPC), sharing the podium with
Representative Jan Meyers (R-Kan.) left, and Pat Hanratty,
Director, Massachusetts Industrial Services Program.
Irene Natividad, Chair of NWPC, is at far right.

politics/self." With such problems to deal with, what makes a Fran, Geraldine, or Jane run?

One answer to that question is *concern about issues.* Most women, like those of the 1960s, get involved in politics because of strong feelings about the state of their community or nation. Good schools, adequate public transportation, jobs for youth and minorities, protection of the environment, women's issues—these are some of the concerns that have led women into politics.

Eleanor Smeal, president of the National Organization for Women (NOW), talks to college groups and urges young women to think about political careers. She wants them to realize that through politics they can affect the laws that affect them. "If 50 percent of state legislators were women, the Equal Rights Amendment would pass immediately," Smeal says, referring to the failure of male-dominated legislatures to ratify a constitutional amendment requiring equal treatment of women under the law.

Along with wanting to have an impact on the laws that govern their communities and nation, a second reason women opt for politics is *a desire to help people.* An officeholder is a representative. She is the spokesperson and the interpreter for those who cannot be present, or who do not know how to make themselves heard. The Speaker of the Sixty-third Session of the Oregon legislature, Vera Katz, began her career in 1973, going door-to-door talking to voters. What she found was citizens talking repeatedly about how poor the schools were at the same time that established politicians kept saying education wasn't an issue. Katz believed the people needed a better voice, and she wanted to be it.

When women do speak up in politics, it has been found that their opinions on public policy are somewhat different from those of men. The Center for the American Woman and Politics (CAWP) at Rutgers University studies women in elective and appointive office. In *Women Make a Difference,* authors Kathy Stanwick and Katherine Kleeman make a forecast.

Regardless of whether women serve in municipal, county, state, or federal offices, whether they are elected or appointed officials, whether they are Democrats or Republicans, they bring different perspectives to the public agenda. Indeed, we believe that women's different perspectives will ultimately reshape the public policy agenda.

It has been observed that women tend to be more concerned with issues affecting women and families such as day care for children, nursing-home care for seniors, programs to aid battered wives, displaced homemaker services, and equal rights legislation. More women than men also oppose nuclear power and the death penalty; more women favor gun control. If significant numbers of women were voting along these lines in state legislatures, city councils and the U.S. Congress, many laws could be altered.

Researchers caution, however, that these observations are only trends. Not enough women hold office at this time for there to be hard evidence about their points of view. More women have to be elected before there can be definite conclusions.

PATHS TO
POLITICAL OFFICE

As of January 1985, 2 states had women governors; 23 women were serving in the U.S. House of Representatives; 2 women held U.S. Senate seats; 41 women were serving in statewide office as lieutenant governors, secretaries of state, state treasurers, and an attorney general; 1,098 women were state legislators; and some 14,462 women held elective office at the municipal and township level. (Figures from CAWP.) This means that more than twice as many women were in office as ten years earlier. How did these women get elected?

There are three typical paths to elective office. One is to follow the party route as a Democrat, Republican, or other. The second is to be active in civic affairs, building a reputation and a network of supporters. The third is to chart an independent course based either on identification with a special issue, or on a direct challenge to the present officeholder.

In many sections of the country it's necessary to go the *party route* because it is the parties who nominate candidates. In Minnesota, for instance, elected officials are frequently active party members. Even town councillors may get their support from the party system. But in California, where an early civil service system cut out patronage jobs as political benefits, parties are far less important. There, many candidates are independents.

Working hard for one's party can give a prospective candidate valuable experience plus a list of probable supporters. In a manual for women running for office, former U.S. Representative Millicent Fenwick of New Jersey told the National Federation of Republican Women how she believed in building support.

> The safest, most reliable way is through the system. This means doing party work in the precincts, welcoming new people, knocking on doors. It goes on all year. It is a terribly hard job if you do it well. You always work under the direction of the executive committee members. And, when the election comes, you conduct yourself with common sense, prudence, zeal, integrity, and good humor. You will achieve a solid basis of work done in the public interest. It is rare that these things will not be noticed or appreciated.

Being active in a party can provide plenty of opportunity to learn practical politics, including the most crucial business—campaign work. Each election year the party sponsors a variety of nominees, all of whom are looking for volunteers to do their stamp licking and other campaign jobs. While it may sound like drudgery, it can be much more than that.

Being active in a campaign is like being behind the scenes in the news. A volunteer with a good assignment can be close to the heart of the action, watching strategy being developed, analyzing issues, and seeing how the politician gets her or his message across. More than 80 percent of the women now in state and county offices worked on someone else's campaign before mounting their own.

The *civic route* to elective office is based on public service. This can be PTA work, League of Women Voters activity, serving on a neighborhood council, or doing other kinds of volunteer efforts that provide a chance to develop knowledge and leadership. Cities and towns also have many boards, committees, and commissions that are filled by appointed citizens. It's possible to learn horse trading while serving on a town budget committee, to see how compromises are made while on a parks advisory board, or to become good at reading laws and regulations while serving on a city civil service commission.

Politics is the only profession for which there is no formal course of study. While many officeholders are college graduates, their knowledge of what the people want and how to deliver it comes not from the classroom but from being out in the community working on community issues.

The third course, the *independent route*, is more difficult to chart than the others. It depends on both the individual and her sense of timing. An independent candidate must have special abilities that fit the needs of the moment. For instance, a businesswoman with experience in economic development may decide she is just what her city needs as mayor in terms of fresh ideas and a change from the old boys' network. If she is very lucky, she may get the support she needs without having been previously active in politics.

While the idea of going it alone may be attractive, it is probably the most difficult way to approach an office. Fenwick, who was schooled in the party system, says that attacking the power structure from the outside, "has been successful and it can be done. But it is not, generally speaking, a good idea." For the most part, she believes that it takes a very special person to put together a strong campaign without relying on traditional backing.

But whether they are party people or civic leaders, there is also the opportunity for women to be active in nonpartisan political groups. These organizations are dedicated to motivating and preparing women for public life, regardless of their other affiliations.

Half of all female state legislators now in office have belonged to the League of Women Voters, a political education and lobbying group. Many have also belonged to local chapters of feminist organizations such as the National Women's Political Caucus and the National Organization for Women. These various groups, composed of individuals who believe in women's rights, inspire women to seek office, sponsor candidates' workshops, provide campaign workers, and even raise money for campaigns.

Another bonus for women is the helping hand women officeholders extend to others. Not only do women hire women on their staffs, but they also freely share what they have learned about the business of politics. Women pols take part in political skills workshops—discussing what they know about fund raising, image building, press relations, polling, and other topics; they interrupt busy schedules to speak to organizations; they counsel individuals who are planning political careers. Most women in office are eager to see their numbers increase.

THE DRAMA
OF GOVERNMENT

Iowa State Representative Minette Doderer has spent more than twenty years in public service. She's a professional in a field she loves. At first her colleagues didn't think Doderer could take the heat of legislative combat, she told the Center for the American Woman and Politics.

> Which just made me tougher and fight harder and try harder. But I love the challenge of the debate, and I love the challenge of disagreement and argument. I learned to be tough because I'm in a tough business. And I learned that anyone will walk over you if you allow them to. And, what's more, they'll enjoy the walk.

After twenty years, Doderer is still filled with zest for her vocation. But what is it that keeps women like her committed to careers in public service? What draws them there in the first place?

By examining the lives of women in American politics, one finds many of the elements of drama: action, suspense, colorful characters, stimulating ideas, second-act losses and third-act wins.

One also finds heroic figures who have served as role models. These are the grand women of history who were the pathbreakers, ahead of their times. These women played a role in the American political process from the very beginning. They set the pace, some of them even before women had won the vote!

★ 2 ★

SETTING
THE PACE

American women were politically active long before they won the right to vote. Early in their history they gained such invaluable political skills as organizing, lobbying, petitioning, and propagandizing. They sharpened and polished those skills in the service of two great causes: the abolition of slavery and women's rights.

In the 1840s, an eloquent and inspired ex-slave adopted the new name Sojourner Truth and took to the open road to preach the cause of "freedom for slaves and freedom for women." From her home in Massachusetts, she traveled as far as Indiana, Missouri, and Kansas. Her fame as a speaker rivaled that of the great abolitionist orator Frederick Douglass.

Truth sensed that social reforms spring from the grass roots—just as surely as all great leaders have sensed that fact. So she went to the people to accomplish the most basic political task of all—raising the consciousness of men and women everywhere, paving the way for the organizers who followed.

The organizers were not far behind. In 1848 Elizabeth Cady Stanton (1815–1902) and Lucretia Mott (1793–1880) called the first meeting on women's rights—a convention held in Seneca Falls, New York. The delegates to that convention issued a "Declaration of Sentiments," which was the opening salvo in the women's rights, or feminist, movement. In their declaration they demanded equal opportunities for women in work and education. At Stanton's insistence they also demanded woman suffrage. As it turned out, the fight for the vote would be the focus of the women's rights movement for more than seventy years. And the first crusading feminists would be the suffragists.

ABOLITIONISTS FIRST

Well into the 1860s, the suffragists were upstaged by reformers who were working to abolish slavery—the abolitionists. Women had always been prominent in the abolitionist movement, but as the Civil War (1861–65) approached, they channeled all their energies into abolitionism, putting their own cause on hold for the duration of the war. Across the North, East, and West, women organized antislavery meetings and demonstrations, wrote and circulated propaganda and petitions, raised funds, and helped slaves escape to Canada, which was an act of civil disobedience.

Because many of the women active in abolitionism were well educated, they excelled as debaters, pamphleteers, and propagandists. Although sometimes equated with lying, propaganda is intended to convince others of the rightness of one's cause and to win their support. The closer to truth propaganda is, the more powerful it will be.

It was a woman, Julia Ward Howe (1819–1910), who wrote the stirring "Battle Hymn of the Republic," which inspired not only the soldiers of the Union, but its supporters at home and around the world. It was another woman, Harriet Beecher Stowe (1811–1896), who produced abolitionism's supreme work of propaganda—the novel *Uncle Tom's Cabin*. Stowe's novel, in Ralph Waldo Emerson's words, "encircled the globe, and was the only book that found readers in the parlor, the nursery, and the kitchen in every household." It convinced men and women everywhere of the evils of slavery, and won their hearts and minds to the cause of abolitionism.

If women gave much to abolitionism, they also gained much from their involvement in that movement. They gained leadership skills from their experience as organizers, coordinators, and fund raisers. Speaking and debating in public, they sharpened their skills in argument and persuasion. Through all these activities—and most of all, through acts of civil disobedience—they acquired a new assertiveness. And almost without realizing it, they built a nationwide, grass-roots network of prospective supporters and allies. The very existence of that network gave women more political clout than they ever before had possessed.

THE MOVEMENT
TAKES SHAPE

Susan B. Anthony (1820–1906), a prominent journalist and feminist, believed that the network women had developed could be held together and enlisted in the cause of women's rights. Foremost among those feminists who won their political spurs in abolitionism, Anthony had served as chief New York agent for the American Anti-Slavery Society. She had also founded and led another abolitionist group, the Women's Loyal National League.

A superb organizer and administrator, Anthony was also an activist of the first rank. More than once, she faced down hostile mobs and audiences with her strong presence and forceful words. True to her Quaker teachings, she believed in resisting unjust laws through acts of civil disobedience. In 1872 she cast a vote in the presidential election. For that act she was arrested, convicted, and fined. Although she refused to pay the fine, the case was carried no further.

In 1868 Anthony and Elizabeth Cady Stanton launched *Revolution*, a weekly newspaper whose masthead bore a rallying cry for suffragists: "The true Republic—Men, their rights and nothing more; Women, their rights and nothing less." In 1869 Anthony and Stanton formed the National Woman Suffrage Association, whose broad objectives included the reform of divorce and labor organization laws.

Later that same year, a major schism occurred in the ranks of the suffrage association. Many of its members rejected Anthony and Stanton's broad social objectives and wanted to focus on winning the vote. Others were put off by their acceptance of any and all supporters, including cranks and eccentrics. In November 1869 the dissidents formed the American Woman Suffrage Association. The most prominent member of the association's executive board was Lucy Stone (1818–1893). It was Stone who raised the money to launch the weekly *Wom-*

an's *Journal* in 1870. Over the years the *Journal* remained the staunchest, most respected journalistic voice of the suffrage movement.

The schism in the feminist movement was healed in 1890, when the two suffragist groups merged to become the National American Woman Suffrage Association (NAWSA). Anthony became president of the new association, and Stone, head of the executive board. The twenty-year division in feminism had held the movement back. But at the same time, women had learned the hard way about political infighting. And they learned the overriding value of unity—the all-important element in gaining and holding power.

In the same year in which suffragism's new, more powerful association was formed, the movement scored a breakthrough victory. In November 1890 Wyoming became the first state to grant women equal voting rights. With that event, suffragism gained a momentum it would never lose.

In 1900 Carrie Chapman Catt (1859–1947) was elected to succeed Susan B. Anthony as president of the association. A brilliant political strategist, Catt developed what came to be known as the "winning plan." The plan was a flexible, two-pronged strategy of working at both federal and state levels to build support for woman suffrage.

In 1915 the association formally implemented the winning plan—and funded it generously, thanks to the nearly $1 million bequest of Miriam Leslie. Catt proclaimed a massive, final drive for a constitutional amendment providing national woman suffrage. She asserted that victory was inevitable: "When a just cause reaches its flood tide, whatever stands in its way must fall before its overwhelming power."

Events soon confirmed the soundness of Catt's strategy and the rightness of her vision. One victory followed another. In 1917 the campaign for woman suffrage in New York State finally succeeded. In 1918 President Woodrow Wilson announced his conversion to the cause of woman suffrage. Tireless lobbying in Congress, directed by Maud Wood Park, and then in state legislatures, finally produced ratification of the Nineteenth Amendment in August 1920. That amendment reads in full:

The right of citizens of the United States to vote shall
not be denied or abridged by the United States or by
any state on account of sex.
Congress shall have power to enforce this Article
by appropriate legislation.

The fight for those thirty-nine words had been a hard one,
demanding the firmest commitment and the highest political
skills. Most of all, it had demanded effective organization and
coordination, which were needed to translate numerical support into political clout. In the course of developing those
skills, women created nationwide, grass-roots networks em-
bracing women in every part of the country. By making women
aware of the interests and values they shared, they created a
feminist community. Such a community exists again today,
long after the fight for the vote was won.

SEVEN TRAILBLAZERS

If American democracy were perfect, it would be unnecessary
to point out the "first woman" or the "first black" or the "first
black woman" to sit in Congress. They would have been there
from the beginning, unnoticed among the others. But the
Founders themselves were the first to admit that they had
created an imperfect democracy, and that it was up to those
who followed to perfect it. Since then, our system has been
improved, if not perfected, each time it has been extended to
include more participants. For that reason, each individual
who scores a breakthrough for one group or another assumes
special meaning.

The trailblazers in women's political history entered the
arena and competed with men for power. They were the first
women to sit in Congress, to serve as governors and big-city
mayors, and to sit on the federal bench.

As the objects of intense public interest and media coverage, they all had to live up to more exacting standards of
performance than their male colleagues. Otherwise, they believed, the door would be closed to other women. Moreover,
they were first to face dilemmas that still confront the female

candidate or officeholder. For these reasons, they are subjects of interest, as well as role models, even today.

Jeannette Rankin

As the first woman to win a seat in the United States Congress, Jeannette Rankin (1880–1973) stuck stubbornly to her pacifist and feminist principles, even when they threatened her survival in politics.

Born in Montana Territory, Rankin was the daughter of a successful rancher and an elementary school teacher. She went to public schools in Missoula, and then to the University of Montana, where she received a B.S. degree with a major in biology. She did graduate work in sociology and economics at the New York School of Philanthropy and the University of Washington. She worked briefly as a teacher and a social worker, but neither career seemed to fulfill her. Only when she became actively involved in the successful Washington state campaign for woman suffrage did Jeannette Rankin discover her vocation in politics. (Various states were granting women the right to vote before the Nineteenth Amendment was passed, making woman suffrage the law of the land.)

In 1912 Rankin worked for suffrage groups in New York, California, and Ohio. In 1913 she became a field secretary for NAWSA, and spent the next two years lobbying for woman suffrage in fifteen states. Her half-dozen campaign trips to Montana helped to win the vote for women there in 1914.

In 1916 Rankin arrived at a crossroads: she could continue to work for national suffrage, she could become a lobbyist for social legislation, or—thanks to the victory for woman suffrage in that state—she could run for Congress from Montana. Choosing to run for Congress, she campaigned successfully as a progressive Republican, calling for woman suffrage, protective legislation for children, tariff revision, prohibition, and "military preparedness that will make for peace."

Jeannette Rankin of Montana
was elected to the House of
Representatives in 1916.

On April 2, 1917, Rankin was sworn in as a member of the House of Representatives, becoming the first female to sit in Congress. Four days later, she had to cast the most important vote of her career—a vote for or against a declaration of war on Germany.

Both Carrie Chapman Catt and Alice Paul, leaders of the prowar and antiwar suffragists respectively, tried to influence Rankin's vote. Her brother urged her to cast "a man's vote" for war. But like many other progressives of the time, including the former secretary of state, William Jennings Bryan, Rankin was a pacifist, opposed to war under any circumstances. "I want to stand by my country," she said, "but I cannot vote for war." Forty-eight other members of Congress voted with her on this historic occasion.

Rankin's antiwar vote had an enormous impact on her long public career. "It was not only the most significant thing I ever did," she later recalled, "it was a significant thing in itself." As the war continued, and American troops suffered heavy losses in France, a patriotic fervor swept the country. Montanans grew disenchanted with Rankin. She could not run for reelection in 1919 because her seat had been eliminated through redistricting.

She decided instead to run for the Senate. Losing the Republican nomination, she stayed in the race as the candidate of the newly organized National party. It was a hopeless campaign from the start, made even more so by Carrie Chapman Catt's endorsement of Rankin's Democratic opponent.

After losing her race for the Senate, Rankin continued to work for feminist objectives, including a federal suffrage amendment. She traveled to Switzerland with social reformer Jane Addams as a delegate to the Second International Congress of Women. For four years, she was field secretary of the National Consumers League. In that post she lobbied Congress for legislation to combat infant and maternal diseases, and directed education campaigns in the Mississippi Valley, aiming to win support for laws improving the working conditions of women. For ten years she worked as a Washington lobbyist and field organizer for the National Council for the Prevention of War.

In 1939, as another world war approached, Rankin decided

to run for Congress again. As a Republican pacifist, she capitalized on widespread antiwar sentiment in Montana, and on the backing of women and labor. She waged a spirited campaign and easily defeated her liberal Democratic opponent.

Back in Congress, Rankin opposed every measure proposed by President Franklin Roosevelt to prepare the country for war. In those votes she was not alone; most of her Republican colleagues shared her isolationist views. Yet when the Japanese attacked Pearl Harbor on December 7, 1941, most members of Congress, isolationists included, became firm supporters of the president.

On December 8, President Roosevelt appeared before a joint session of Congress to deliver his "day of infamy" speech and to request a formal declaration of war. In the vote on that request, Jeannette Rankin stood alone in the Congress and, ultimately, in her home state.

Rankin had been out of the national limelight for more than two decades when she became an active opponent of the Vietnam War. In 1968, when she was eighty-seven years old, she led the Jeannette Rankin Brigade of several thousand women to Capitol Hill to protest the war. Not long after the successful protest, she announced her intention of running for Congress again—so that those who opposed the war would "have somebody to vote for." But the dream was not to be. Rankin's long career ended as it had begun, in a flurry of traveling, public appearances, and demonstrations.

Rankin will be remembered as a representative guided by moral convictions, rather than by practical or career considerations. In office she remained true to the values of pacifism and feminism, sometimes at the cost of slighting the values and preferences of the people who had elected her. But as she saw it, lawmakers were chosen for their judgment and vision, and not for the favors they could do. Rankin never wanted to be a successful politician so much as she wanted the opportunity to affirm her values for the world to see.

Margaret Chase Smith

Early in her career in the United States Senate, Margaret Chase Smith (1897–) was asked what she would do if she woke up one morning to find herself in the White House. "I'd go straight to Mrs. Truman and apologize," she said, "then I'd leave by the back door."

Smith's remark was a reflection less of modesty than of political realism. In her time, as recently as the 1960s, neither of the two major parties was ready to put a woman on a national ticket, not even if she was the first woman to be elected in her own right to the U.S. Senate. Smith, nevertheless, received several votes for the presidential nomination at the Republican National Convention of 1964, becoming the first woman nominated for the presidency by a major party.

Born in Skowhegan, Maine, Smith went to work as an elementary school teacher after graduating from high school. She also worked as a telephone operator and a reporter, and became active in business circles and Republican politics. In 1926 she became president of the Maine Federation of Business and Professional Clubs. In that post she developed a network that would prove invaluable in her political career.

In 1930 Margaret Chase married Clyde H. Smith, a local political figure and co-owner of the *Skowhegan Independent Reporter*. After her marriage, she became even more active in politics, serving for several years as a member of Maine's Republican Committee. When her husband was elected to the House of Representatives in 1936, she went to Washington as his secretary.

When Clyde Smith died in 1940, his widow was chosen in a special election to complete his term. Almost immediately she displayed the independent judgment that would characterize her career. Breaking with the isolationism of her Republican colleagues, Smith voted with the Democrats for the Selective Service Act, which President Roosevelt argued was essential to military preparedness.

Respecting her for her independent positions, Smith's constituents elected her in her own right to a full term later in 1940, and after that, three more times. During her eight years in the House, Smith served on the Naval Affairs and the Armed Services committees, concerning herself especially with the status of women in the armed forces. She played a major role in the passage of the Women's Armed Services Integration Act of 1948, which gave women equal pay, rank, and privileges.

In 1948 Smith ran a successful campaign for the Senate,

winning by a record plurality. She was reelected by large majorities in 1954, 1960, and 1966, serving in the Senate longer than any woman has since. Her seniority entitled her to important committee assignments in which she had an opportunity to shine. These included membership on the Armed Forces, Appropriations, Government Operations, and Rules committees. On the Armed Forces Committee, Smith shattered the stereotypes of women's capabilities held by her Senate colleagues with her firm grasp of military hardware, strategy, and budgets.

On domestic issues, Smith was generally liberal, voting to support most major social welfare programs. But she voted with the conservatives on issues of national defense and security. She publicly denounced Senator Joseph R. McCarthy for his campaign of slander—at a time when most of her Republican colleagues feared McCarthy and refused to speak out. Smith received frequent citations as woman of the year, and the *Newsweek* press poll rated her as the most valuable senator for 1960.

In 1972 Smith ran her last campaign. Confident of her standing with the voters in Maine, she was preoccupied with the divisive debate over the Vietnam War. She stayed in Washington that fall, returning to campaign in her home state only twice. Her opponent made much of her age and health, and in a surprising upset, he succeeded in unseating her.

Like Jeannette Rankin, with whom she served in the House, Margaret Chase Smith had a mind of her own. She, too, believed that neither her party nor her constituents had a monopoly on wisdom. But on that fateful day when President Roosevelt asked the Congress for a declaration of war, the two women in the House of Representatives stood poles apart. Unlike Rankin, Smith believed that World War II was not only necessary, but morally justifiable. Each woman was moved by a different vision of the world—one sign of the diversity among women coming into politics.

Shirley St. Hill Chisholm
No black woman sat in either house of Congress before Shirley Chisholm (1924–). And no woman had ever been nominated for president by the Democrats before her.

Born Shirley St. Hill in Brooklyn, New York, Chisholm was the daughter of parents from British Guiana (now Guyana) and Barbados. She spent part of her childhood in Barbados and then returned to Brooklyn, where she attended high school and graduated from Brooklyn College in 1946.

Chisholm had planned a career as a teacher or social worker. While she taught in a New York nursery school, she studied education at Columbia University's Teachers College, which granted her a master's degree in 1952. The next year she became director of a child-care center in Manhattan, and consultant to the New York City Bureau of Child Welfare (now the Division of Day Care).

Chisholm's growing involvement in community problems led her into politics. "So many of those problems couldn't be solved without fighting city hall," she said. Her command of Spanish, her skills in local organizing, and her popularity with the predominately black and Puerto Rican people of her district gave her a ready-made political base.

In 1964 Chisholm ran for the New York State Assembly and won. In each of two reelection campaigns that followed, she increased her margin of victory substantially. In 1968, confident that her record in the Assembly gave her a strong base, she decided to run for the U.S. House of Representatives from the newly created Twelfth Congressional District, which centers on the impoverished Bedford-Stuyvesant neighborhood of Brooklyn.

In the race that followed, Chisholm easily defeated her Republican opponent, James Farmer, the distinguished former chairman of the Congress of Racial Equality (CORE). Her first act in Congress was to protest her assignment to the House Agriculture Committee as irrelevant for an urban Representative. The party leadership then placed her on the Veterans Affairs Committee. A little later, she voted for Representative Hale Boggs over a black representative, John Conyers, for majority leader. After his victory, Boggs gave Chisholm a place on the prized Education and Labor Committee.

In Congess Chisholm became an effective and respected spokesperson for minority rights and urban needs. In 1972 she entered several Democratic presidential primaries. At the party's national convention she received 151 votes for the presidential nomination, a feat no other woman before or since has achieved.

Chisholm prided herself on her practical approach to politics. "I'm a pragmatic politician," she told a reporter; "I believe that compromise is the highest of all arts." She added that "some blacks are not politically sophisticated enough to understand the pragmatic reasons behind my moves. Blacks can't do things on their own, nor can whites. When you have black racists and white racists, it is very difficult to build bridges between communities."

Since Chisholm's time, four other black women, all Democrats, have served in the House. They are Yvonne Brathwaite Burke of California and Barbara Jordan of Texas, both of whom served from 1973 to 1979; Katie Hall of Indiana, who served from 1983 to 1985; and Cardiss Collins of Illinois, who was elected in 1973 and still serves in 1986.

Frances Perkins

Frances Perkins (1882–1965), the first female Cabinet member in history, is also the only Cabinet member who once was a member of the Socialist party. Her membership was brief, however. After a few months of listening to "visionary speeches," Perkins decided once and for all that the best social remedies were practical ones.

Born in Boston, Perkins grew up in a comfortable, middle-class, Republican household in Worcester, Massachusetts. She attended Worcester Classical High School, and studied chemistry and physics at Mount Holyoke College, which granted her a B.A. degree in 1902.

In her senior year at Mount Holyoke, Perkins read Jacob Riis's *How the Other Half Lives*, which she described as "a profound influence" on her life. In the same year, Perkins heard a speech by Florence Kelley, general secretary of the National Consumers League. Perkins later recalled that it was Kelley who "first opened my mind to the necessity for and the possibility of work which became my vocation."

After college, Perkins did graduate work in economics and sociology at the University of Pennsylvania and Columbia University, where she earned her master's degree. Her first full-time job was teaching physics and biology at a school in

Lake Forest, Illinois. In her free time, she worked at several Chicago settlement houses, including Jane Addams's Hull House. Among other volunteer tasks, she made the rounds collecting wages for workers who had been cheated, she visited the homes of the poor, and she was introduced to the labor movement.

Moving to New York City, Perkins took a job as secretary of the New York Consumers League. Working closely with Florence Kelley, she drew attention to sweatshop conditions in bakeries, and lobbied the state legislature in Albany for industrial reform. She found time to teach college courses, march in suffragist demonstrations, and speak on street corners in behalf of the suffragist cause.

In 1911 Perkins witnessed the Triangle Shirtwaist Company fire in which 146 garment workers perished. The tragedy left an indelible imprint: images of young women jumping to their deaths from window ledges. Moved to action, Perkins resigned from the league and went to work for the Committee on Safety of the City of New York. On behalf of the State Factory Investigating Commission, she traveled through New York State identifying employers who were jeopardizing the health or lives of their workers through negligence. As a result of the commission's efforts, the New York State legislature passed a number of progressive measures.

In 1918, Perkins accepted an $8,000-a-year appointment as a member of the New York State Industrial Commission, becoming the highest paid female state employee in the country. She took charge of the Bureau of Mediation and Arbitration, reorganized its factory inspection division, and went into the field to settle strikes.

Perkins had openly backed the presidential ambitions of Franklin D. Roosevelt, the governor of New York, long before he won the nomination. Yet when she learned that prominent women, including Jane Addams, were urging President Roosevelt to name her as his secretary of labor, Perkins resisted, suggesting that a female trade unionist be named. But Roosevelt insisted, calling her "his most loyal friend" and a person who had "no axe . . . to grind." Relenting, Perkins said, "I had been taught long ago by my grandmother that if anybody opens a door, one should always go through."

As Roosevelt's New Deal took shape, Perkins rebuilt the U.S. Department of Labor. Under her guidance, the Immigration and Naturalization Service was purged of racketeers, the Bureau of Labor Statistics was expanded, the Women's and Children's bureaus turned in highly competent performances, and an upgraded Federal Mediation and Conciliation Service gained the confidence of most labor leaders.

Perkins was the only Cabinet secretary to serve President Roosevelt in all four of his administrations. After his death, she served briefly in President Harry S. Truman's Cabinet before becoming a member of the Civil Service Commission, a post she held until 1952. In 1957 she accepted a professorship in Cornell University's School of Industrial and Labor Relations. She taught there until 1965, the year of her death.

Throughout her career, Perkins was modest about her own accomplishments. But her imprint on wages and hours legislation, Social Security, and the Department of Labor had been enormous. She had made her way through a world of men without losing a strong sense of her own identity, or her commitment to the interests of women in general.

Florence Ellinwood Allen

The daughter of pioneers in the Utah Territory, Florence Ellinwood Allen (1884–1966) would become a pioneer of a different sort—the first woman to sit as a judge on a federal court, and the first to sit on a court of last appeals anywhere in the world.

Allen attended high school in Ohio, while her father served in Congress as Utah's first Representative in Congress. She received her B.A. and a master's degree in political science from Western Reserve University in Cleveland, Ohio, before entering the University of Chicago Law School. She interrupted her law studies in 1910 to go to New York and work for the New York League for the Protection of Immigrants. In New York, she lived at the Henry Street Settlement House, where she met leaders of the suffragist and social welfare movements. At the same time, she continued work for her law degree, which she received in 1913 from New York University.

Admitted to the Ohio bar in 1914, Allen opened her own office in Cleveland, volunteering her services to the Legal Aid

Society and the Woman Suffrage Party. She became active in local Democratic politics, making the connections that led to her appointment as assistant prosecutor of Cuyahoga County in 1919.

After ratification of the Nineteenth Amendment, Allen announced her candidacy for common pleas court judge. Members of the Woman Suffrage party carried her petitions. She won the support of church and labor groups, unions, and both political parties. She ran first in a field of candidates that included nine men. As the first woman on any court of general jurisdiction, she set about improving judicial administration.

In 1922, Allen ran for the Ohio Supreme Court with strong, statewide support, including aid from sixty-six Florence Allen clubs. In her Model T Ford, she took her campaign to the grass roots. Winning by a large majority, she became the first woman in the world to sit on a court of last resort. She was reelected by a wide margin in 1928.

In 1934 friends and supporters of Allen's from labor, education, and reform groups backed her nomination to the Sixth Circuit Court of Appeals. Unlike the state judgeships she held, this is a federal judgeship whose incumbents are appointed by the president. President Roosevelt was convinced of the wisdom of ending the male monopoly of the federal courts, and he appointed Allen to the judgeship. She became the first woman to sit on any federal bench of general jurisdiction, retaining her seat for twenty-five years—the last as chief judge.

Allen's most notable decision as a federal judge concerned the constitutionality of the powers granted to the Tennessee Valley Authority (TVA). Private electric companies from nine southern and border states had sued TVA, challenging its authority and decisions. The decision hinged on the consideration of masses of technical data, and the long 1937 trial tested Allen's legal and administrative abilities.

Judge Allen's decision upheld the right of TVA to buy transmission lines from private companies, to sell electricity generated by its dams, and to build new dams. Upheld by the U.S. Supreme Court, Allen's ruling had widespread implications for New Deal public works programs. The public attention that she received at the time encouraged speculation that she would be elevated to the Supreme Court. But Allen had correctly predicted in a letter to a friend, "That will never happen to a woman while I am living."

Florence Allen's aim as a judge was to perform so that the public and her peers would find female authority appropriate. At the end of her career, she was confident that she had lived up to that goal: "Judges who were at first opposed to women officials accepted us when we handled our work steadily and conscientiously."

Ella Grasso

The first woman ever to become a governor on her own, and not as the wife of a previous incumbent, was Ella T. Grasso (1919–1981), a liberal Democrat who became the governor of Connecticut in 1974.

Born Ella Rosa Giovanna Oliva Tambussi in Windsor Locks, Connecticut, she was the daughter of Italian immigrants. "My father was a baker," she recalled, "so we always had enough to eat. We were comfortable, because we had no major illnesses and he could work." Proud of her working-class origins, Grasso boasted to a reporter, "It took me years to learn that 'youse' is not the plural of 'you.' "

On the basis of her good grades at Saint Mary's Roman Catholic High School in Windsor Locks, Grasso was admitted on scholarship to the elite Chaffee School in nearby Windsor for her college preparatory work. From Chaffee she went to Mount Holyoke College, where she majored in sociology and economics, made Phi Beta Kappa in her junior year, received her B.A. degree magna cum laude in 1940, and her master's degree in 1942.

During World War II, Grasso served as assistant director of research in the Connecticut office of the federal War Manpower Commission. Through her active membership in the League of Women Voters, she developed an interest in politics, and, as she later said, "a real understanding of issues." She became a protégée of the state Democratic party chairman, and a dedicated party worker.

After several years of service to the party, she ran for the state legislature, where she served two terms. In 1958 she was elected Connecticut's secretary of state, a post she held for twelve years. In that office she became one of the best-known politicians in the state. Her office on the first floor of the State Capitol building in Hartford became a "people's lobby," where ordinary citizens came to air their grievances and seek advice.

On the national level, Grasso served as Democratic committeewoman, and as cochair of the resolutions committees at the Democratic National conventions in 1964 and 1968. At the 1968 convention, the overriding issue was the war in Vietnam. The issue overflowed into the streets of Chicago, where police clashed violently with peace demonstrators. Grasso was instrumental in pushing through the convention a minority report opposing continued United States involvement in Vietnam. And she was among those who walked out of the convention to protest the tactics used by Mayor Richard Daley's police force to suppress antiwar demonstrations.

In 1970 Grasso ran for Congress, winning with 51 percent of the vote. When she ran for reelection two years later, she won nearly 70 percent of the vote. In the House of Representatives, she served on the Education and Labor Committee and the Veterans Affairs Committee, supporting liberal legislation. Bravely, she voted for defense spending cutbacks, despite the millions of dollars that would have gone to the defense industry in Connecticut.

In 1974 Grasso announced her candidacy for governor, despite the reluctance of many state party leaders to endorse her. Even so, she trounced other Democratic hopefuls in a key primary and was nominated by acclamation at the Connecticut Democratic Convention. Early in the campaign, noting the attention she was receiving as a woman candidate, she said, "The judgment will be made of me as an individual, on the basis of what I have accomplished in my career in public life."

While distancing herself from the women's liberation movement, Grasso was careful to explain she was not unsympathetic to "women's lib." "It's done a great deal in a short time to provide equal opportunity for women, and I feel I've been a beneficiary. Four years ago I might have had some difficulty in advancing a viable candidacy as a woman, but it's a non-issue now." Her observation proved correct on Election Day, when she swamped her opponent.

As governor in hard times, Grasso faced the most difficult challenge that a politician can face: cutting expenses and balancing the budget. In her inaugural address, she warned the citizens of Connecticut to prepare for austerity, saying, "Our state is in disarray. The financial condition of state government today is unsound. A balanced budget and an operating surplus do not exist." Bowing before strong popular resistance to a state income tax, Grasso was nevertheless determined to restore Connecticut to solvency.

The budget presented by Governor Grasso to the legislature the next month was for a record $1.43 billion. To close a prospective gap of $150 million between that figure and actual state revenues, Grasso proposed a 1 percent rise in the sales tax, among other measures. Looking for ways to economize in state spending, she began with herself, rejecting a $7,000 increase in her $35,000 salary. Within four years, an inherited deficit had been turned into a surplus. And Grasso had maneuvered skillfully enough to retain the support of the many fragmented groups that made up her constituency.

Running for reelection in 1978, Grasso first had to fight off a challenge from her lieutenant governor in the Democratic primary. She then went on to win reelection by a large majority. But during the first year of her second administration, Governor Grasso revealed that she had cancer and would undergo surgery. After a courageous battle with the disease, she died in 1981, shortly after resigning from office.

Grasso's achievement in becoming the first woman governor was a breakthrough. She demonstrated that a woman can operate in the environment of state politics, where machines play tough. As a governor, she was the first woman to hold the highest executive office that women have so far held. As chief executive of Connecticut, Ella Grasso left a legacy of responsible administration in challenging times.

Jane Byrne

Jane Byrne (1934–) thrived as a politician in one of the toughest environments of all—Chicago. For nearly fifty years Mayor Richard Daley ruled that city with an iron hand, giving its citizens more or less what they wanted, and making the city work, but taking many shortcuts when it came to observing democratic procedures. Never in fifty years had anyone challenged Daley's machine before Jane Byrne did. And ironically, she claimed to be Richard Daley's heir.

Byrne came from an upper-middle-class background, the second of six children and the oldest of four girls. Born between two brothers, she has said, "I did whatever they did. That's probably why I never had any hang-ups about the difference between a man's job and a woman's job." She was educated in Catholic schools, including Barat College of the Sacred Heart in Lake Forest, Illinois. There she majored in chemistry and biology, earning her bachelor's degree in 1955. Once, she had planned to become a doctor, but gave up that ambition when she married William P. Byrne and became a mother. Her husband, a Marine Corps pilot, was killed on active duty while their daughter was still a baby.

In 1960 Jane Byrne became active in John F. Kennedy's campaign for president, serving in a salaried post of the Kennedy for President organization in Chicago. Prominent Kennedy supporters were so impressed with her performance that they offered her a job with the new administration in Washington. But, not wanting to uproot her daughter, Byrne remained in Chicago, taking education courses at the University of Illinois, receiving her teacher's certificate, and teaching part time in Chicago public schools.

In 1964 Mayor Daley appointed Byrne to a relatively minor position with the Chicago antipoverty program. He urged her to prove herself in grass-roots work so that more-seasoned volunteers and political regulars would not disapprove if he named her to a city post. Over the next four years, Byrne learned the ropes of city politics, and in 1968, true to his word, Daley appointed her commissioner of consumer sales, weights, and measures.

Determined to rid her department of corruption, Byrne promptly fired several staff members. Faced with protests from the city's aldermen, Daley defended her action. She moved on to make her department a strong advocate of consumer justice, pushing through a ban on phosphate detergents, a new system of grading meats, a requirement that gasoline retailers post easy-to-read octane ratings, and a public exposure of dishonest auto repair practices.

When Mayor Daley was recovering from a stroke in 1974, Byrne attacked the aldermen who seemed to be planning eagerly to succeed him as "little men of greed" and "political vultures." After the mayor's death in 1976, the men she denounced lost no time in exacting revenge. They removed her from her post as cochair of the Cook County Democratic Committee, but permitted her to stay on as comissioner of consumer sales in Mayor Michael Bilandic's administration.

A rift existed between Byrne and Bilandic, widening beyond repair when she accused him of "fraudulent and conspiratorial action" in "greasing" the way for a taxicab rate hike. Following the disclosure of Byrne's accusation, the mayor fired her. Making an issue of Bilandic's supposed dishonesty, and of the deteriorating condition of the city, Byrne challenged him in the Democratic mayoral primary of 1978.

Claiming to be "Mayor Daley's rightful political heir," Byrne campaigned doggedly, playing on the contrast between Chicago's longtime reputation for efficiency and its current condition. Her slogan became, "The city that works doesn't." On primary day more than 800,000 Chicagoans went to the polls, electing Byrne by the narrow margin of 15,000. When the primary outcome was certain, she declared in a voice hoarse from ten months of campaigning: "The machine killed itself. I'm going to run it straight, and I'm going to run it clean. There will be no clout."

In the general election in April 1979, Byrne won 82 percent of the vote and carried all fifty of Chicago's wards. It was a triumph greater than any that Mayor Daley had known.

As mayor, Byrne was determined to increase the efficiency of city government while, at the same time, cutting its budget. She carried out shake-ups of the city's sanitation and police departments, and replaced several commissioners and other top officials with people she felt would be more cooperative. She ordered department heads to fire deadweight employees regardless of their political patrons.

In 1983, as she approached the end of her first term in office, Byrne was challenged in the Democratic primary by

Richard M. Daley, the son of the late mayor, and Harold Washington, a black man. With the white vote split between Byrne and Daley, and blacks voting overwhelmingly for Washington, the outcome of the race seemed inevitable. After a racially divisive campaign, Washington was elected mayor. Since then Chicago has been divided by the conflict between the mayor and the all-white city council.

In July 1985, with the Chicago skyline as a backdrop, Jane Byrne held a news conference to announce her candidacy for reelection in 1987. "For two years we've sat," she said. "We've sat and watched our city become paralyzed. I know I just can't sit by and just watch " By announcing her campaign two years before the next mayoral election, Byrne hoped to freeze out other candidates.

No one knows what to expect in the marathon that Byrne anticipates for the mayor's office—or whether she will find the stamina and money to see it through. But the country will watch with fascination, knowing that Chicago poses the ultimate proving ground in American politics.

In the careers of these seven political trailblazers—Rankin, Smith, Chisholm, Perkins, Allen, Grasso, and Byrne—striking contrasts stand out. Two of the seven sat on the same bench in the House of Representatives on that day in 1941 when President Roosevelt asked Congress for a declaration of war. One of them voted for war; the other voted against it. Two of these women were rising stars at the 1968 Democratic National Convention in Chicago. One of them approved of Mayor Daley's brutal tactics in handling protestors; the other led a group from the convention hall in protest.

Even from the beginning, it was not possible to stereotype the values or policy positions of women. This small group of seven includes Republicans and Democrats, liberals and con-

Jane Byrne, who succeeded Chicago's mayor Richard Daley, was the first woman to head the government of a major American city.

servatives, big spenders and budget cutters, hawks and doves. And yet, underlying their diverse values and positions was a common concern—a concern for the individual.

The trailblazers shared a talent for seeing policy in concrete terms—in terms of its impact on men, women, and children. As a result, their achievements were gains for individuals who otherwise might have been neglected—workingwomen, working mothers, working children, women in the armed forces, the urban poor, the consumer. The collective accomplishments of just these seven trailblazers broadened our political agenda forever. Their careers confirm the proposition "Women make a difference."

★ 3 ★

O'CONNOR AND FERRARO

With Jane Byrne's mayoral victory in 1979, women had won nearly every elective and appointive office on the federal, state, and local levels of government. Untouched were the presidency, vice presidency, and the Supreme Court. In the early 1980s, however, two women—Sandra Day O'Connor and Geraldine Ferraro—made significant gains.

The first of the remaining hurdles in women's race for political equality was cleared on December 5, 1981. On that day, in the high-ceilinged marble chamber of the Supreme Court, the justices assembled for the opening of their 1981–82 term. The marshal of the Court rapped his gavel on a wooden block and cried: "The honorable, the Chief Justice and Associate Justices of the Supreme Court of the United States. Oyez, oyez, oyez. All persons having business before the honorable, the Supreme Court of the United States are admonished to draw near."

As he spoke, Chief Justice Warren E. Burger and the eight associate justices, wearing black robes, filed in through the red velvet curtains behind the bench. For the first time in history, the "nine old men" included a woman. The presence of Sandra Day O'Connor on this day transformed a 191-year-old ritual into a precedent-shattering event.

As a justice on the Supreme Court, O'Connor could have a greater impact on American lives than any other woman and few men so far have had. Appointed for life, justices often sit on the Court for twenty or thirty years or more, making decisions that shape citizens' most basic rights and opportunities. For the fact is, the Constitution means what the Supreme Court says it means. And every president, every political party, and every powerful group in American society wants to see justices appointed to the Court who will be sympathetic to their own interests and ideology.

POLITICS AND
THE SUPREME COURT

Historically, presidents have chosen Supreme Court justices for their politics more than for their judicial talents. The practice is not necessarily bad if it does not lead to the appointment of mediocre judges. In fact, it is one important way in which the Supreme Court is at least indirectly responsive to the voters.

By appointing O'Connor to the Supreme Court, President Ronald Reagan hoped to make good on two campaign promises: to advance women in government, and to reverse the activist and liberal role taken by the Supreme Court in the 1950s and 1960s, under Chief Justice Earl Warren (1953–69).

Under Warren, the Court outlawed official racial segregation in public schools, set strict national standards to protect the rights of criminal defendants, required the equal apportionment of state legislatures and the House of Representatives, legalized abortion, and ruled that prayers and Bible reading in public schools are unconstitutional.

President Reagan and other conservatives believed that the Warren Court exceeded its rightful powers in some of these decisions. They wanted a Supreme Court that would reverse those decisions, a Court that would interpret the Constitution more narrowly, stopping short of social reform.

The conservatives were also aware that justices of the Supreme Court have often confounded the presidents who ap-

Sandra Day O'Connor posed with
former Chief Justice Warren Burger
on the day she was sworn in as the first
woman Supreme Court Justice.

pointed them with unpredictable decisions. After Oliver Wendell Holmes ruled against President Theodore Roosevelt in a key antitrust case, the president, who had appointed Holmes, ranted, "I could carve out of a banana a judge with more backbone than that." Said President Dwight Eisenhower about his selection of Earl Warren: "The worst damn fool mistake I ever made."

For that reason, O'Connor's supporters, her detractors, and Supreme Court watchers in general have scrutinized her opinions more than any others, searching for signs of the kind of justice she will be.

A broad range of political liberals, moderates, and conservatives supported O'Connor's nomination and appointment. Feminists were generally pleased; the president of the National Organization for Women (NOW), Eleanor Smeal, hailed the choice as "a major victory for women's rights."

But spokespersons for the New Right felt "betrayed" by the appointment. They charged that O'Connor was a closet supporter of the Equal Rights Amendment, and that she favored freedom of choice on abortion. The Reverend Jerry Falwell, leader of the Moral Majority, declared that all "good Christians should be concerned about the appointment."

Of greater importance than her stand on abortion were O'Connor's qualifications to serve on the Court. On that point, legal scholars familiar with her record were in agreement: she is a brilliant lawyer who learns quickly. The decisions she handed down while sitting on the Arizona appeals court revealed a good mind, strong skills in argument and legal reasoning, and a generally conservative approach to the law—that is, a reluctance to go beyond existing precedents, interpreting the law freely. Beyond that, her experience in a state legislature gave her a working knowledge of the lawmaking process that none of the current justices on the Supreme Court can claim.

FROM THE LAZY B
TO THE LAW

The first woman Supreme Court justice was born on the Lazy B, a 260-square-mile cattle spread on the Mexico–Arizona border. The ranch has been in the Day family for more than a hundred years, three decades before Arizona became a state. Because there were no schools nearby, Sandra spent much of her youth with her grandmother in El Paso, attending private and public schools there.

She finished high school when she was sixteen years old and then did something her father had longed to do: attend Stanford University in California. There she completed her undergraduate work and law studies in only five years. She won membership on the prestigious *Stanford Law Review*, where she met her future husband, John, as well as William Rehnquist, who was appointed to the Supreme Court in 1972.

O'Connor's first job was that of deputy county attorney in San Mateo, California. After that, while her husband served in the U.S. Army, she worked as a civilian lawyer for the Army Quartermaster Corps in West Germany. In 1957 the O'Connors returned to the United States and settled in Phoenix, where the first of their three children was born. Sandra O'Connor tried running her own law firm for a year, but then gave it up for a five-year stint as housewife. During those years she was a joiner—president of the Junior League, adviser to the Salvation Army, auxiliary volunteer at a school for blacks and Hispanics, and a member of private clubs. "Finally," she recalls, "I decided I needed a paid job so that my life would be more orderly."

For four years O'Connor worked as an assistant attorney general of Arizona. Then, in 1969, she was appointed to fill a vacancy as a state senator. She ran for that seat and won it in 1970 and 1972. In 1972 her seventeen Republican colleagues in the Senate elected her majority leader.

As majority leader, she revealed a talent for persuasion. When she talks about her legislative achievements, she dwells on tax relief, flood-control funding, and the restoration of the death penalty. But she also favored passage of the Equal Rights Amendment in 1972, and two years later attempted to put ERA before the voters in a referendum.

In 1973 she cosponsored a bill that would make "all medically acceptable family-planning methods and information" available to anyone who wanted them. Those methods, her critics charged, might be interpreted to include abortions.

O'Connor remained silent on that charge, although she has said that she finds abortion "personally repugnant."

As a legislator, O'Connor was careful about the letter of the law. Once she offered an amendment to a bill to insert a missing but important comma. She read up on issues and pending legislation more thoroughly than most of her colleagues, gaining an advantage over them. According to another state senator, "It was impossible to win a debate with her. We'd go on the floor with a few facts and let rhetoric do the rest. Not Sandy. She would overwhelm you with her knowledge."

A STERN BUT FAIR JUDGE

As the end of her final term as a state legislator approached, O'Connor had reached a crossroads. She had to choose between politics and the law. She is more comfortable with the law, she has said, "because it is always changing." She ran for and won a judgeship on the Maricopa County Superior Court. As a trial judge, her colleagues recall, O'Connor was stern but fair. At least twice she advised defendants to get new lawyers because their present lawyers were unprepared.

After a middle-class mother of two infants had pleaded guilty to passing bad checks totaling $3,500, she begged O'Connor for mercy. She said that her husband had abandoned her, and that her children would become wards of the state. O'Connor sentenced the woman to five to ten years in prison, saying, "You should have known better." When she returned to her chambers, she broke into tears. In another case, she ordered the death penalty for a twenty-three-year-old man found guilty of murder for agreeing to kill another man for a fee of $3,300.

When state Republican leaders urged O'Connor to run for governor in 1978, she turned them down. Instead she accepted a seat on the Arizona Court of Appeals. There she made no landmark decisions, but compiled a record of solid decisions that were rarely reversed by a higher court. She had served for three years when, in June 1981, she was interviewed by the U.S. attorney general's staff as a candidate for the Supreme Court appointment.

O'Connor's experience as a legislator, a state government lawyer, and a trial and appellate judge were impressive. She was also described as tough on law-and-order issues and reluctant to rule against the police on technicalities. One deputy attorney general wrote: "She was the right age, had the right philosophy, the right combination of experience, the right political affiliation, the right backing. She just stood out among women." The president agreed, and O'Connor was appointed.

ON THE HIGH COURT

Decisions of the Supreme Court are widely publicized, but very little is known about how the Court works or how justices arrive at their decisions. By custom justices rarely grant interviews, and never write memoirs. On only a few occasions have they departed from this custom, and even then, they have revealed very little.

Procedures of the Court are highly formal, having changed very little over the past two centuries. Federal attorneys who appear before the Court must wear morning clothes. A lawyer arguing before the Court usually has one half hour to make his or her case. Five minutes before the time is up, a white light flashes; when a red light flashes, the lawyer must stop. Justices often use up precious time by interrupting the attorney for questions. O'Connor is known to question lawyers aggressively.

On Fridays the justices meet in conference to decide what cases they will hear, and to discuss and vote on pending cases and appeals. By tradition the justices shake hands as they file into the oak-paneled conference room. Newcomers are told to call the others by their first names, but they can be intimidated by the legendary standing of their colleagues. Chaired by the chief justice, these meetings are so secret that not even the justices' law clerks are permitted in the room.

Sometimes sharp disputes erupt among the justices. Rarely do they all agree on the interpretation of the law or on the correct decision. Their disputes, of course, reflect underlying philosophical and ideological differences. As each case is discussed and reduced to its basic principles, the liberals and the conservatives on the court tend to form two groups. Majority and minority positions emerge.

So far O'Connor has sided rather consistently with two

conservatives on the Court—former Chief Justice Warren E. Burger and conservative activist William H. Rehnquist, who replaced Burger as chief justice in July 1986. This lineup, observers say, is exactly what President Reagan had in mind when he appointed O'Connor.

On at least two occasions, however, O'Connor parted company with her two conservative colleagues to take a more liberal position. On the first occasion, she joined with five other justices to find that Title IX of the Federal Civil Rights Law, which bars discrimination on the basis of sex or race in federally funded education programs, also forbids bias in school employment. On the second occasion, O'Connor broke with Burger and Rehnquist in her opinion that Mississippi violated the law by setting up an all-female nursing school. In her written opinion, O'Connor warned other justices against making "traditional, often inaccurate, assumptions about the proper roles of men and women."

"NOW IT'S OUR TURN"

Geraldine Ferraro lost her bid for the vice presidency, but nevertheless succeeded in clearing another hurdle for women in politics. As far as women are concerned, Ferraro's nomination is more important than her defeat. Now that a major political party has nominated a woman for vice president, no major party can exclude women from consideration in the future. Such is the power of precedent in politics.

Geraldine Ferraro's story embodies, in the words of reporter Maureen Dowd, "the Cinderella myth, the American dream and the feminine mystique." Gerry was named after a brother, Gerard, who died when he was three years old. When she was eight, her father died, and her mother went to work crocheting beads on dresses. She scrimped to send Gerry to an expensive Roman Catholic girls' school, Marymount, in Tarrytown, New York, and then to Marymount Manhattan College, where she earned a B.A. degree in 1956.

Gerry wanted to become a doctor but became a teacher instead "because women didn't become doctors in the fifties." Bored with teaching elementary school, she attended Fordham Law School at night, one of two women in a class of 179.

Admitted to the New York State Bar in 1961, she worked part time as a lawyer in her husband's real estate firm throughout the 1960s and early 1970s. Like many local lawyers trying to build a practice, she was active in a Democratic club, getting to know her working class neighborhood and the local party leaders. In 1974 she became a full-time lawyer, winning an appointment as assistant district attorney in Queens. In 1975 she moved to the newly created Special Victims Bureau, established for charges involving abuse of the elderly and children and for rape cases. She became head of the bureau in 1977.

When she decided to run for Congress in 1978, Ferraro thought she had earned the backing of local party leaders, yet they balked at the idea of a female candidate. She ran anyway, standing on street corners in the sweltering heat, asking people to sign her own petition. She ran harder than anyone had expected, and won victory by a comfortable 10 percent margin. She increased that margin substantially in each of her two campaigns for reelection. As a strong vote getter in a highly diverse district, Ferraro attracted the attention of her party's leaders.

PUTTING CONSTITUENTS FIRST

At the outset of her first term in office, Ferraro made it clear that the interests of her constituents were her main concern. She told biographers Rosemary Breslin and Joshua Hammer: "I didn't go down to Washington to represent the women of this nation. I ran, and was elected, not as a feminist, but as a lawyer. I didn't go to Washington to speak for the poor of this nation. I am not a bleeding heart, a sob sister. My campaign slogan in 1978 was 'Finally, a tough Democrat.' I represent a conservative, middle-class, hard-working constituency, and I went to Washington to represent them."

Ferraro won respect in the House of Representatives by being what a fellow New York congressman called "just one of the guys." As a freshman, she played "the game," in which newcomers are expected to defer to their seniors. She cultivated party leaders by willingly performing more than her share of legislative and party scut work. She so impressed the Speaker of the House, Tip O'Neill, that he rewarded her with choice assignments—secretary to the House Democratic Caucus, and a member of the Democratic Steering and Policy Committee and the Budget Committee. O'Neill said, "She has been a regular since the day she arrived."

Having won the confidence of the party leadership, Ferraro was determined to prove herself. She went into "immersion" to acquire expertise in the subjects and issues that demanded her attention. In her memoir she recalls being intimidated at the first hearing of the Public Works Committee that she attended: "I sat listening to the male members asking questions during the testimony, and every one of them sounded like an expert. 'Is it in their genes that they know all this stuff about decibel levels?' I asked my staff." No, her staff told her; it was sitting through hundreds of hearings on this subject that gave a member expertise. To compensate for the experience she lacked, Ferraro pored over the transcripts of earlier hearings before attending any future committee meeting.

A RISING STAR

After her reelection in 1982, Ferraro set her sights on the powerful Budget Committee, which has the last say on all expenditures by all branches of the federal government. Because she was still a very junior member, her chances were slim. Yet, she lobbied and traded votes skillfully enough to win her seat and to emerge as a real contender for power.

Budget Committee Chair James Jones recalled that Ferraro conscientiously attended every committee meeting as budget resolutions were being hammered out. Jones said, "She listens before she talks. On whatever areas were special to her she spoke her mind. She won more than she lost." Having played an important role in shaping the budget, Ferraro used her ties with the New York congressional delegation and the women's caucus to win support for the package. Jones said, "She's a team player in that she helps build coalitions to pass whatever budget we develop."

Ferraro enjoyed playing the role of vote-swapping, pork barrel politician, and she played it well. She voted for dairy supports to help out Representatives from farm districts. In appreciation for that vote, a Missouri-based dairy group later contributed to her campaign fund. To win points in her conservative, mostly blue-collar district (where the credits of *All in the Family* were filmed), she parted ways with other Democrats to vote for tuition tax credits for parochial schools, and against mandatory busing. On most other issues, she voted the party line.

Ferraro was credited with getting federal funds for New York City's water tunnel project and larger federal reimbursements for the protection of diplomats. She was tireless in her attention to the special interests of her highly ethnic district—from defending Soviet Jewish dissidents, to denouncing Turkish policies, to opening a hotline to provide updates on conditions in Poland, to commemorating the contributions of German-Americans. At the same time, she supported legislation of special interest to children, women, and senior citizens. For a while, she cochaired the congressional women's caucus.

Six years of solid performance won her the respect of peers, party leaders and constituents alike. By 1983 it was clear to everyone who followed politics that Geraldine Ferraro had a great deal going for her. A year later she was the right person, and it was her time.

ENTER TEAM A

In November 1983, Ferraro's administrative assistant, Eleanor Lewis, invited her to dinner with a small group of politically active women. They wanted to discuss her political future with her. Over a Chinese take-out dinner, they told her that they had two goals: first, to create a Democratic ticket strong enough to beat Ronald Reagan; and second, to fill the vice presidential slot on that ticket with a woman.

They told Ferraro that they had reviewed the backgrounds of every possible woman vice-presidential candidate and concluded that she had the best prospects. They offered to become her personal political-advocacy group, in return for her active and public advancement of the idea of a female vice president.

While her chances of winning the vice presidential nomination seemed slim, Ferraro respected the judgment of these professionals. She agreed to their plan.

In phase one of Team A's strategy, the dual objectives were, first, to convince the male-dominated media to take the concept of a woman vice-president seriously; and second, to win the support of influential politicians. Both objectives were accomplished with ease. Over the next few months, writers such as Jane O'Reilly of *Time* and columnist Judy Mann of *The Washington Post* began advancing the idea in print. And leading contenders for the Democratic presidential nomination, including Edward Kennedy, Walter Mondale, and Gary Hart, publicly declared their support for the idea.

In phase two of Team A's strategy, the names of specific candidates for the vice-presidential nomination were to be advanced. Ferraro agreed to have her name mentioned as a possibility. Beyond floating her name, Team A aimed to enhance Ferraro's credibility in the eyes of party leaders. They began to lobby to have her appointed platform chair at the upcoming Democratic National Convention in July 1984.

"Always the realist," writes Ferraro, "I was thinking about what a breakthrough my role as Platform Chair would be for women and that it would put me in a more visible position to campaign effectively against Reagan." But Team A had set its sights on nothing less than the vice-presidential nomination, and saw the role of platform chair as a stepping stone for Ferraro. Unknown to her, they began dropping her name in discussions about the vice presidency.

THE SELECTION PROCESS

For two weeks the country watched and waited as Walter Mondale, his nomination for president assured, interviewed an impressive lineup of vice presidential contenders. They included the Jewish woman mayor of San Francisco, the Hispanic mayor of San Antonio, the black mayor of Los Angeles, and the congresswoman from Queens. Each hopeful had the backing of powerful groups; each group pressured Mondale unrelentingly. In Ferraro's corner were Governor Mario Cuomo of New York and House Speaker Tip O'Neill.

Mondale calculated the benefits each candidate could bring to the national ticket. Besides Ferraro's proven appeal to the voters, she would balance the ticket regionally. But would the voters accept a woman? Was it time? These questions were more or less unanswerable, although there was evidence to support the choice of a woman. In 1969, 50 percent of Americans surveyed in a Gallup poll said that they would consider voting for a female presidential candidate. By 1983 that percentage had risen to 80.

Among party activists, support for a female candidate was even higher. A final survey of delegates to the Democratic National Convention in July 1984 revealed that they overwhelmingly favored the choice of a woman for the vice presidential nomination. Of all the possible women candidates, Ferraro stood at the top of the list. The survey was rushed to Walter Mondale as he arrived in San Francisco on July 9. Mondale was impressed.

Two days later, Fritz Mondale called Gerry Ferraro in her hotel room to ask, "Will you be my running mate?" Ferraro stuck her head out of the bedroom and said to a staff dying of curiosity, "How does it feel to be part of history?" In Queens, the news spread like wildfire. Walter Mondale had called Gerry Ferraro and asked her to run for vice president. Gerry had said yes. Another door had opened.

OFF TO A BAD START

The campaign got off to a bad start. First, Ferraro's staff prepared a press release promising the release of her husband's tax returns, as well as hers. Her husband, however, had agreed to release only the financial statement required by law. Later he released his returns, and questions about his finances plagued Ferraro's campaign to the very end.

Friction between Ferraro's campaign staff and Mondale's was another problem. Before the campaign had begun, Mondale's campaign manager had prepared Ferraro's campaign schedule without consulting her or her staff. He was trying to push her into an active role before she had organized. Meeting with Mondale, Ferraro held her ground, even though he "became beet red with anger." Appealing to his sense of fairness,

Geraldine Ferraro, the first woman candidate for vice president, salutes delegates at the Democratic National Convention in 1984.

she said, "As your running mate, I want to be consulted, rather than listen to your staff telling me what I have to do."

" 'They're not used to dealing with a woman,' I continued, 'but they're going to have to learn. . . .' Fritz seemed surprised. I explained that his staff would not have been so presumptuous had they been dealing with a senior male senator—or any man." From that day on, the Mondale staff transmitted all their messages and inquiries to Ferraro through her staff. "At least now," Ferraro writes, "our two campaigns would give the appearance of understanding each other." But the friction persisted, and there were "constant disagreements" between the two staffs.

TAKING THE
TOUGHNESS TEST

Like the first woman to compete for every other office, Ferraro faced extreme skepticism about her competence. In a television debate with her opponent, Vice President George Bush, she turned in a strong performance. Many who watched believed that she had bettered Bush in her grasp of issues and policies. But even after the debate, her qualifications to be commander in chief were questioned.

"Are you strong enough to push the button?" asked Marvin Kalb on *Meet the Press.*

"I could do whatever is necessary to protect this country," Ferraro replied.

Behind the question was a larger issue. Ferraro writes: "It was so endlessly annoying to be presumed as weak and indecisive simply because I was a woman. And the question about 'button pushing' was such a simplistic one. The discussion was never about whether force should be used only when every other avenue is exhausted, or whether or not I had the knowledge and the intelligence and fortitude to move toward arms control negotiations. . . . There I was, less than three weeks from Election Day, still undergoing a foreign policy exam. . . ."

From the very beginning, Mondale and Ferraro knew that they were fighting an uphill battle. They were running against one of the most popular presidents in history. No incumbent president had ever been turned out of office in a year of economic growth. The country was not at war. Short of a major disaster, nothing could have stopped Ronald Reagan from winning a second term.

THE LEGACY

Was she devastated by the loss? "No," Ferraro writes; "there was the undeniable pride in making history. And there was the legacy I could leave to other women with leadership aspirations. . . . We have proved we have the stamina to get through a campaign, to stand up for our beliefs in a national televised debate, to articulate the issues. . . ." As for the next female candidate on a national ticket, Ferraro writes, "Perhaps the style of her campaign will be less important and the substance will get the attention it deserves."

Summing up the Ferraro candidacy in *The New York Times*, Maureen Dowd wrote:

. . . Ferraro, despite her flaws, usually handled her role as the first woman to run for the Vice Presidency with grit, intelligence and humor. She refused to follow the advice of aides who wanted her to get contact lenses or wear man-tailored suits, and expertly walked a fine line between sensitivity and toughness. She wrote a new chapter on women in politics, balancing her roles as mother, wife, daughter, woman and candidate with a graceful instinct.

★ 4 ★

IN TOWN HALLS AND CITY COUNCILS

The press paid a lot of attention to the appointment of Sandra Day O'Connor to the U.S. Supreme Court and to the vice presidential candidacy of Geraldine Ferraro. Local officials Jane Byrne, Dianne Feinstein, Kathy Whitmire, and Carol Bellamy are also names in the national news. Byrne, Feinstein, and Whitmire have commanded attention as mayors of major cities—Chicago, San Francisco, and Houston. New Yorker Bellamy was president of the nation's largest city's city council. But with less fanfare, thousands of women throughout the country are working equally hard in town halls and city councils, dealing with many of the same problems.

Sharon Jean, borough assembly member from Soldotna, Alaska, says that entering local office is an initiation into the realities of the political process. In *Names, Notes and Quotes for Alaskan Women*, Jean told about the difference she found being first a liberal advocate for community services and then being an elected official who must deal with a broader range of problems and decide how such services can be provided.

When one is an advocate for women's rights or organizing a women's center, they are working outside of the system, sort of gnawing at the inside to get their needs met. But the tables turn when a liberal is in office, has to compromise and make tough decisions.

It is interesting, when you are on the outside, you think anything is possible. When you get inside, some of the things are clearly not possible and you must deal with this. There is a different level of knowledge one needs to operate within the system.

The good news, Jean says, is that anyone can learn the system by participating. And on the local level, there are countless opportunities.

Local politics has been called "the meat grinder of life." All measures necessary to provide for the citizens' health, welfare, and safety on a daily basis pass through local legislative channels. It is here that officials are most visible to the public, and it is here that issues hit closest to home.

If she lives in a small town, a representative knows little privacy from the day she steps into office. Weeding her garden, shopping at the supermarket, having a quiet dinner in a restaurant—all can be interrupted at any time by a citizen with an idea or a complaint. The reason for such intrusions is simple: a public official's decisions affect many aspects of her neighbors' lives. As a council member, commissioner, school board official, or other, she has her fingers on vital issues.

To understand the scope of local offices, it's helpful to review the basic purpose and organization of government at this level.

FORMS OF GOVERNMENT

Local government is closest to the community on a daily basis. It is usually the town or city that monitors the purity of our food and water; it may take care of trash and garbage; it may provide a bus or rail system; it may give fire and police protection; it may plan road systems and neighborhood development; it may run the local airport; it may create parks and recreational programs; it may sponsor health clinics; it may run the schools. From local government come most of the laws that make a community an agreeable place to live.

There are several forms of local government; common ones include the mayor-council plan, the commission plan, and the city manager plan.

In the *mayor-council* plan, voters elect both the mayor and council members who may represent specific districts or be elected at-large. The council decides on local laws, or ordinances, and the mayor is charged with seeing the laws carried out. The mayor appoints the heads of different executive departments of city government and administers their work. Under this plan, the mayor is a full-time city employee, while councillors are usually paid a small salary for part-time service.

Under the *commission* plan, commissioners are elected to represent individual districts, or they may be elected at-large. Commissioners head one or more departments of government; they also make city laws and see that they are enforced. Commissioners are often professionals in related fields. A water commissioner, for instance, may well be a sanitary engineer.

Under the *city manager* plan, voters elect a small council which makes ordinances and decides general matters. The council in turn appoints a manager to enforce the laws. The manager selects the heads of departments, reports to the council on local needs, suggests how public money should be spent, and so on. The council can accept or reject the manager's ideas.

Village and *town* governments exist where there are not enough people to form a city government. This is common in New England, where many townships cover from 25 to 40 square miles. The village or town is governed by a board or council elected by citizens at an annual town meeting. Other elected officials are a mayor, town clerk, tax assessor, and treasurer.

County government in many states is the most powerful form of local government. County officials run a court system; oversee elections; build and maintain schools; keep official records of birth, death and taxes; administer welfare and health programs; build bridges and repair roads. The county is governed by a board of commissioners or supervisors who are elected. In most states, a county sheriff and tax assessor are also elected.

Judges may be elected to preside over local courts, rather than being appointed by the council, commission, or governor. School board members are elected, as are many planning commission panels.

From school boards to county seats, women are making gains in local government. At the beginning of 1985, Alaska could boast more women in local government (borough) than any other state. Women held 36 percent of all borough assembly seats (a borough is like a county). Hawaii, California, and Arizona followed with women counting for more than 20 percent of the representatives on county governing boards. In Maryland, Indiana, New Hampshire, New Jersey, Delaware, and Florida, one in every ten representatives was female. (Based on CAWP figures.)

Women were also increasing their presence on city councils. While their numbers do not adequately reflect the female population (53 percent), they do show a steady improvement in representation. And besides serving on local assemblies, women are assuming more leadership by chairing these bodies.

Among the hundred largest cities, seven have woman mayors. One of these is Kathy Whitmire of Houston, Texas. Whitmire's story shows the range of problems with which a mayor must deal.

MAYOR KATHY WHITMIRE: THE CHALLENGE OF LOCAL GOVERNMENT

Houston, Texas, is the nation's fourth largest city, stretching more than 25 miles across. Since it exploded with the oil boom of the early 1970s, Houston has been plagued with urban problems caused by rapid growth. It offers a massive challenge to any who would rule it. Kathy Whitmire both manages the city and chairs the city council as Houston's first female mayor.

Whitmire told the *Women's Political Times* why she wanted to serve Houston.

> I ran for office at a time when the day to day responsibilities of city government were simply not being taken care of. And that was the platform that I ran on, that we need a business-like approach to managing city government if we are going to expect basic services. So that has had to become my highest priority, getting city government to work for the people here, to get the potholes fixed and get the sewer system to be adequate.

But of course, those same issues are further reaching, because the economic vitality of our city, the job opportunities for our people, depend upon our ability to have a transportation system and to have a sewage treatment system that doesn't pollute our waterways. So the issues are a bit larger than the mundane sounding tasks of fixing the sewer lines and the potholes.

Houston is a large and complex business, according to Whitmire. She has stressed her ability to bring modern management to a city that some say was too long in the hands of a good old boys' network that ran the city like a club. As a CPA (certified public accountant), Whitmire is a professional manager. Her knowledge of money matters has enabled her to attack the most difficult problems, such as reorganizing fiscal operations.

Whitmire's straightforward approach to issues also helped her attract a talented staff to work on Houston's problems. She pushed for civil service reforms and worked to get approval for development ordinances to help get the city's runaway growth under control.

But near the end of Whitmire's first term in office in 1983, a newsmagazine predicted she would not be reelected in spite of her good management. The oil boom which made Houston prosper had been followed by an oil glut, and city revenues were down by $20 million. Whitmire proposed laying off four hundred city workers to avoid raising property taxes, a move sure to create new enemies. At the same time, Houston voters said no to a $2.3-billion bond issue for a heavy rail system she was promoting as a solution for the city's severe traffic problems.

The police were also testing Whitmire's authority. Many were upset when she hired a black man to head the police force as public safety commissioner. Later, when the cost of health insurance went up and pay raises were slim, police officers took their anger right to the top. They stormed a city council meeting, demanding changes. Whitmire held fast, but it was a difficult experience.

When Hurricane Alicia tore up Houston in 1983, overturning homes and shattering windows on the downtown skyscrapers, it seemed that Whitmire's cup was running over with trouble. But she managed a speedy recovery for Houston from the hurricane, and rode out her problems with city workers. Thanks to Whitmire, Houston kept its first-class bond rating (enabling it to borrow money for projects), put 15 percent more police on the streets, and began to achieve more orderly growth. When Whitmire faced reelection, she could do so with a smile, even adding some humor to her campaign.

The same magazine that prediced Whitmire's failure liked to call her "Tootsie." It seems there was a Hollywood movie about an actor who got a job on a television soap opera playing a female administrator. The actor, played by Dustin Hoffman, was called "Tootsie" in his role. With curly hair and big glasses, Whitmire and Hoffman's character looked somewhat alike, so the mayor was dubbed "Tootsie."

When a designer's list of America's 10 Worst Dressed Women came out, the author got on the bandwagon and named Hoffman and Whitmire number 10. Instead of railing against the silliness, Whitmire grabbed the idea and used it in her campaign. "Tootsie is a 10!" her buttons said. She was reelected by a handsome margin, smiling all the while.

Knowledge of good management practices helped Whitmire succeed as chief executive in Houston's government. But while she had been trained in management and knew how to work with business problems, it was in dealing with different departments of city government and as head of the city council— dealing with other elected representatives—that she said she had to learn new skills.

Working with a group of representatives requires special knowledge. Not only parliamentary rules must be learned to be effective at meetings, but also informal methods of gaining cooperation must be sought. These skills are the same, no matter what the size of the city.

MAYOR FRAN ULMER: BUILDING CONSENSUS

In 1983, Fran Ulmer was elected mayor of the City and Borough of Juneau—a unified government serving 27,000 people in the capital of Alaska. In Juneau's council–city manager form of government, the mayor's duties include chairing the city/

borough assembly and representing the capital to the public. In a typical week the mayor's calendar had her greeting the San Francisco 49ers football team, taping a television spot, entertaining important visitors off cruise ships, holding open office hours to talk to citizens about their concerns, presiding over an assembly meeting, plus sitting in on various subcommittees.

But it is behind the scenes that much of the business of government goes on, and it was there that Ulmer sharpened one of her most valuable skills—consensus building.

Consensus is necessary for the smooth administration of government. It means that the majority of a panel, such as a committee or city council, have found a proposal mutually satisfying. With consensus, the group approaches the law, policy, or procedure with positive feelings and an intention to support the outcome. Consensus is important because it indicates that a community can pull together toward a common goal. Consensus shows respect for people's feelings and values. Ulmer believes that women are particularly well suited for consensus politics.

> Generally speaking, women are raised as peacemakers. They don't particularly care for conflict and strife. Most women are interested in bringing people together, rather than playing "high stakes poker." If I see two polarized positions, I approach it with the idea of finding a common denominator.

Discovering how a law or ordinance can be written to suit more than one interest requires patient communication. Meetings, conversations, telephone calls, breakfasts, lunches, dinners, recreational events, all are opportunities to work on an issue. As Ulmer describes it, helping groups of people unite in their goals is a sensitive process. It is not unlike being a traveling diplomat. "You must find out what they think is important, go back to the other people, take their temperature, find out what they are willing to change."

Part of Ulmer's campaign for mayor included a promise to create neighborhood councils, giving them the right to advise the assembly of their wishes on specific legislation. Like

Houston, Juneau has grown quickly, and there is fear that neighborhoods may be hurt as new roads and housing units are built. While the idea of neighborhood councils was popular with average citizens, some builders and other business persons feared the councils would rigidly oppose more development. It took eighteen months for Ulmer to get a neighborhood council ordinance passed because of resistance. Consensus was finally achieved through a slowly worked out compromise, giving business interests their due while still empowering the councils. The first vote on the neighborhood council ordinance was 3 to 3, with abstentions. The final vote was 8 to 3, which indicated a good base of support.

A successful leader must also know how to use the media in forging consensus, Ulmer says. It's possible to give an idea to the press and let the radio or newspaper stimulate public discussion. This can help persuade representatives to change their minds, or to give a little on an issue. Another tactic is to call an influential person and give her or him information which can be used to help persuade elected officials to get together and agree.

In the interest of communication, an official can choose to be available to citizens at their request. Ulmer decided to do this—to keep public office hours and also to make her home telephone number available. While open hours can be taxing and open communication means loss of privacy, it also helps to strengthen the community because there is a sense of someone responsive at the helm.

At the end of her two-year term as mayor, Ulmer was urged by many Alaskans who had watched her performance as mayor to use her experience as a stepping-stone to higher office—either running for the state legislature or for lieutenant governor. The skills of diplomacy, patience, and consensus building she practiced in local office were seen as being needed on a statewide level.

Mayor Fran Ulmer of Juneau, Alaska, offers strong leadership for a rapidly developing city.

Ulmer may prove to be one of the women in politics who develops a career ladder beginning with local office. But for many, serving the community is an end in itself, with many officeholders serving for ten years or more on local boards, commissions, and councils.

COUNCIL MEMBER
BARBARA ROGERS:
EARNING CREDIBILITY

Barbara Rogers is in her second four-year term on the Cupertino, California, City Council. Before being elected, she was head of the Public Safety Commission, overseeing police services. Working with police officers helped sensitize Rogers to some of the problems a woman can have in gaining credibility in local government.

Rogers believes that if a woman knows her subject and is interested in doing a good job, these will communicate themselves. But she must also show a willingness to listen and learn, and she must not approach a problem by attacking what she sees.

> I think that a great many groups who tend to be conservative and traditional, such as police, often regard women who are successful as being knee-jerk liberals. They are often suspicious of them. They don't want to communicate too much because they're afraid it will be used against them by this far-out woman who doesn't understand how the real world works. They think she'll just take anything they give her and use it against them. That kind of perception has to be overcome.

To help establish a relationship with the officers who serve the community, Rogers has ridden on patrols with them. This gives the men a chance to become better acquainted, while at the same time giving her a better understanding of the public safety problems affecting the city. Rogers feels that spending time with the officers is evidence that her interest in their problems and opinions is sincere. "It's not phony."

But being credible is not just being agreeable and attentive. As a council member, Rogers sometimes has to make unpopular decisions. Part of her political development has been getting used to standing steady when citizens get upset and look for someone to blame for their problems.

When citizens are irate, they often take their woes to town halls and city councils, looking for relief. When Rogers chairs the city council, she is respectful of everyone's right to her or his point of view. No matter how emotional a person might become, or how poor a speaker she or he might be, Rogers always sees that each person is heard. One of her chief assets as a leader is the ability to let citizens air their grievances, while still keeping to the agenda and getting the council's regular business done. "We don't get off on too many tangents, or get waylaid by the emotional posturing people sometimes do."

Because Cupertino, which has a population of 38,000, is in the shadow of much larger cities—San Francisco and San Jose—it doesn't get too much press coverage, "unless we do something that's flamingly different." However, there is still the need to inform residents of local happenings and to keep them in touch with council business. As part of her concern about local government, Rogers edited a city newsletter for six years beginning with her first term in office.

Cupertino Scene is not a slick publication. It's a folded 8½-by-11-inch sheet, including a questionnaire citizens can send to city hall to get written answers to their questions. In it are listed all the actions the council has taken, explained in words people can understand instead of governmentese. General interest events are also described, such as chamber of commerce business, an arts festival, a story about a citizen who helped make an arrest, and so forth.

Another way city council business is communicated to the public is by having council meetings cable-cast on a regular basis. This allows Rogers and other council members to achieve greater visibility and to express their views directly to a broad audience. There is also the inevitable one-on-one contact of voter to official. "It's still a small town," Rogers says. "Every time I go to the grocery store someone says, 'About this—.' "

As a public speaker, Rogers works at improving her skills.

She belongs to a group called "Toastmasters," which gives her the chance to practice speechwriting and delivery. Rogers says there is always something new to learn to be effective. But she doesn't think this is any more true of women than of men.

> Men have the same problems. It's perceived that they automatically do everything well, and they don't. A lot of men perspire and struggle as much or more than I did. And they go through a lot of the same soul-searching. But women still think that everything comes easily to them. I don't think it does.

Women tend to make a mystique of politics, Rogers says. They don't realize that the work they do in other areas is not unlike the organizing and project management that goes on in government. "Women often sell themselves short."

Whether it's in campaigning or laying out their accomplishments as officeholders, Rogers says that women have to learn to toot their own horns.

COUNCIL MEMBER JOANNE COLLINS: FORMING COALITIONS

When Joanne Collins decided to run for city council in Kansas City, Missouri, she realized she would have to build a broad base of support.

> It was of necessity that I had to build a coalition. I'm a Republican in a predominately Democratic district, so I had to overcome partisan politics. Then there's being a woman—the so-called "unfitness" of women for public office, dealing with all male decision-makers. Those kinds of things forced me to look at the organizations I belong to.

As a professional volunteer and black community activist, Collins found that she belonged to dozens of groups. In each of these groups she knew people who had special skills to offer

Joanne Collins relies on support from diverse interests in her Kansas City council district.

her campaign. So instead of running as a Republican with a Republican staff, she ran with broad-based bipartisan support.

Reaching for help from a variety of sources worked in Collins's campaign, and it has become a habit in her work on the council, too. She looks to community groups to find answers to problems and to give support where it's needed.

> Most of our problems are very complicated and individuals need to be pooled from all areas of concern. When I'm dealing with the homeless or a youth problem—of not being able to render the services to the youth who need it—I find that I not only have to go to my county, my state, but I need to go to my community youth centers and churches, and in some cases to the individuals themselves who need the services, and say to them, "What do you feel would be the best way to solve your particular problem?"

Collins says that you can't always find the answer to a problem by dealing with one organization. By putting together a committee representing labor, business, neighborhood associations, schools, and so on, an official increases the odds of finding an acceptable solution. She also builds a coalition to support the solution, because each of the committee members can go back and encourage their organizations to help make the outcome successful.

In gathering groups together to work on common issues, Collins has found it is useful to talk in terms of the problem, ignoring where the Republicans or Democrats stand. This is because some people don't like to think of themselves as dealing with "politics." But most people respond to problems that are posed in terms of community welfare.

Because she is good at stirring up interest and motivating people, Collins takes part in community education programs, such as Round Robins. One of her goals is to get local residents to rethink their particular form of local government, to make sure they have the best kind of representation they can get. For example, if all the representatives are chosen at-large, some neighborhoods, such as those composed of the poor or minorities, may have no representation. Collins encourages locals to work to change the structure of government, if that is what is needed.

But Collins's vision does not end at Kansas City limits. She is involved with the National Political Congress of Black Women (NPCBW), a group created by former Congresswoman Shirley Chisholm. Here Collins finds expression for her national and international concerns.

The NPCBW is a bipartisan group which hopes to affect issues such as child care, taxation, peace, and international relations. The women in it are studying the status of black women everywhere, trying to find ways to prevent the growing poverty which impacts black women and children more than any other population group. In addressing such problems, "We are looking for support from all strata of society," Collins says.

Networking to solve problems, as Collins does, is a distinguishing feature of women in politics. Few women in office consider themselves as Democrats or Republicans only. They often belong to women's groups as well, where they look for support for common concerns.

SCHOOL BOARD MEMBER
MARY BUSCH:
STRIVING FOR EXCELLENCE

Local government reaches into many areas of the community, not the least of which is the school system with its own board of elected officials. The school board's job is to create educational standards and find the means to maintain them. It is not unusual for school board members to also be experienced as professional educators themselves.

Few careers in politics show more focus than that of Mary Busch, a black leader who works both in the field of education and as a school board member. From the time she graduated as valedictorian of Crispus Attucks High School in 1958, to her position today as one of Indianapolis's most respected public officials, Busch has steadily acquired credits in the field of education. As a teacher, school administrator, and school board leader, her aim has always been to achieve excellence.

Busch was first elected to the Indianapolis Board of School Commissioners in 1975, the year she earned a doctorate in

Mary Busch brings to her position on the Indianapolis Board of School Commissioners a deep understanding of education issues.

elementary education. Since then she has served as president and vice president of the board, and been elected to the governing panel of the National School Boards Association. Some of the difficult issues she has dealt with are desegregation, school-parent relations, the effect on public schools of tuition tax credits, and the board's impact on school curriculum.

During Busch's tenure, Indianapolis schools have been cited for their commitment to excellence. But maintaining quality has become increasingly difficult, according to Busch. Cutbacks in both federal and state support for educational programs are seriously damaging urban schools, she says.

Programs designed to help minority and poor students—such as preschool programs, Head Start, and lunch assistance—have been crippled by the loss of federal and state dollars. Classrooms have suffered from budget cuts. Some two hundred teachers were laid off in Indianapolis in 1985. For the first time in Busch's experience, the school board found itself having to go to the public and ask for money to try to hold the line.

In campaigning for increased property taxes to aid the schools, Busch has had to try to convince the general public of the long-term value of good education. She has had to show people that stable schools are a good investment. According to Busch, "Excellence costs money," but it's worth it.

> At some point we have got to start looking at education as an investment in the future of this country rather than looking at it as a mere expenditure of funds. It really gets down to having to ask yourself, How much of America's talent can we afford to continue to waste? You've got to think about how it will be in this country when these students who are coming up now are going to be our leaders.

Getting the public to raise property taxes for school revenues requires a major effort. Six months before the voters' referendum, Busch has to start talking to everyone from small parent groups to the mayor, business leaders, and other movers and shakers. She tries to get them to keep their eyes on the future. What happens if Indianapolis doesn't have a quality school system? Are businesses going to move in? Are there going to be jobs? Will crime rates go up if students are not in school and learning?

Being a school board member can be a hard-hitting job. People don't want to hear about problems and the need for more money. But Busch has a reputation for straight talk and dedicated problem-solving. Her district, which is black and white, lower and middle income, trusts her. The people of Indianapolis listen when she talks.

Busch believes that being a single person is an asset given the huge demands of public service. Her job as director of community services for Indiana Central University commands her days, the school board work takes the rest of her time, along with serving on the boards of such groups as the Indiana Black Expo, the Indianapolis Urban League, and Operation PUSH for Excellence.

Like so many women in politics, Mary Busch is willing to work time and a half to be a conscientious leader and a good communicator. In her case, she uses the power of her position to try to increase opportunities for the powerless—for minorities, the poor, and the young. This, she believes, is necessary in the pursuit of excellence for all.

★ 5 ★

IN STATEHOUSES
AND STATE
LEGISLATURES

When Ann Richards decided to run for Texas state treasurer in 1982, her campaign staff had a problem. In their view, voters wanted their elected officials to be nice people, but experience had taught them that no woman could attack her opponent and still look "nice." So instead of talking about the incumbent's supposed lies and misdeeds, they talked about his job performance.

Again, there was a problem. No one wanted to listen to the fine points of information about the state treasurer's job. So again they changed tack, according to campaign manager Jane Hickie.

> We talked about computers—incessantly. On television, over the radio, in mailings, we repeated the same message: "We need to get this office out of the quill pen era, and into the era of what Texas is today!"

The Richards people repeated their message until the public finally bought it. The result was that their candidate won the primary and went on to win the general election with 63 percent of the vote. Richards's election as a woman to the office of state treasurer was a first for Texas. It also placed her in the company of those women who have been elected to the highest state offices.

Two women were governors at the beginning of 1985; five served as lieutenant governors; thirty-four were elected to statewide executive offices, including Arlene Violet of Rhode Island who, in 1984, became the first woman elected attorney general in any state.

In state legislatures, women held 14.7 percent of all seats, that number having tripled in fifteen years. One-third of the legislators in New Hampshire were women; and other states with more than 20 percent women in their legislatures were Vermont, Wyoming, Colorado, Washington, Maine, Connecticut, Arizona, Florida, and Oregon. (Figures from CAWP.)

Whatever her position, the goals of a woman in state office are similar to those of a local official. She must raise her sights from the particular to the general good, balancing the needs of her constituents with the needs of other citizens. She must collaborate on actions designed to secure the safety, health, and property of the people.

To understand more about the actual business of women in state office, it is necessary to know something about the nature of state government.

OBLIGATIONS OF THE STATE

The character of state government is decided by each state's constitution. This document lists the rights of the people, tells how government is to be organized, sets out rules for local governments, and gives the principles to be followed in organizing the state.

One of the most important obligations is to protect public health through licensing health professionals, examining food and drugs, controlling alcohol sales, and providing hospitals and school health programs. The state also contributes to education, appropriating money for schools and deciding what subjects should be studied. The state maintains a militia, generally in the form of National Guard units. It regulates businesses which are potentially hazardous, such as mines and factories. It builds and maintains roads and other public facilities. It inspects gas, water, and other public-service companies for safety. It regulates work hours and establishes minimum wages.

Elected officials are found in all three branches of state government—executive, judicial, and legislative. The *execu-*

tive branch includes the governor, lieutenant governor or secretary of state, treasurer, auditor, attorney general, and various commissioners and members of the governor's cabinet.

The *governor*'s chief duty is to see that the laws of the state are carried out. To do this, the governor advises the legislature on the state budget and promotes specific pieces of legislation and programs such as economic development. The duties of the *secretary of state* or *lieutenant governor* vary widely, but often she or he keeps official records and supervises elections. As chief legal officer, the *attorney general* advises the governor and represents the state in the courts. The *treasurer* manages income from taxes, licenses and fees, and pays the state's bills. The *auditor*, or a comparable official, examines all books kept by public officers.

The *judicial branch* is a system of law courts with authority over civil and criminal cases. Each state constitution determines the number and kind of courts that exist and how judges must be selected. In some states judges are appointed, while in others they are elected.

In every state except Nebraska, the *lawmaking branch* is made up of two separate groups. One house is called the Senate; the other is the House of Representatives, House of Delegates, or Assembly. In some states, representatives are elected from areas comparable to counties, while senators are elected from larger districts that contain one or more counties. The scheme varies from state to state.

In the forty-nine states with bicameral legislatures, laws are made in the same general way. Any member of either house can bring forward a bill she or he wishes to have made into law. This bill is sent to a committee. After study, the committee may decide to sit on the bill and do nothing, or it can report back to the house and suggest that the bill be passed. Legislators then have a chance to talk for or against the bill before a vote is taken. If a majority votes for the bill, it then goes to the other house where the same steps are taken.

After the bill has passed both houses, it is sent to the governor. If the governor likes it, it will be signed. If not, it will be vetoed. The bill can survive the governor's veto only by being approved again by both houses—by a significant majority of votes.

The governor is a powerful figure. The ultimate success of legislation can hinge on the governor's values and vision for the welfare of the state. Two women presently hold this important position—two women who worked their way up through the ranks of service, one being devoted to her party and the other to special issues.

GOVERNORS
MARTHA LAYNE COLLINS
AND MADELINE KUNIN:
SUBSTANCE AND EXPERIENCE

Martha Layne Collins, a Kentucky Democrat elected in 1983, and Madeleine Kunin, a Vermont Democrat elected in 1984, have different points of view on several major issues. But one thing the governors share is a strong background in politics beginning at the grass-roots level.

Collins, who first learned to deal with the public as "Miss Kentucky Derby," entered politics when she was a high school home economics and math teacher. She worked for the local Democratic precinct, where her devotion got her elected to the state central committee. Friends would often find her working late at night, her two children asleep on the floor of the committee office.

Collins's willingness to do any job and her ability to do it well earned her the attention of former governor Wendell Ford, who became her mentor. His advice helped shape her career.

In 1975 Collins was elected clerk of the state court of appeals, an exacting administrative position. Four years later she was elected lieutenant governor, which represented another step up the political ladder. When she decided to go for the top, she had firm party support for her systematic and cautious approach to issues. She spoke up about her opposition to abortion and her approval of the death penalty, conservative positions that many Democrats in Kentucky appreciated.

Collins's husband, Bill, was her chief fund raiser. He collected some $5 million for his wife's campaign. Like most married women in office, Collins says she never could have succeeded without her husband's wholehearted support.

In Vermont, when Madeline Kunin ran for governor, her husband, a doctor, handed out leaflets and wore a sandwich board promoting his wife on the streets of Burlington. As it turned out, every token of support counted in Kunin's victory. She ran a very tight race, defeating her opponent by a vote of 116,245 to 112,505

The celebration that followed the victory delighted the new governor. Folk dancers clogged in the statehouse lobby, chamber musicians held forth on the floor of the House, and horse-drawn sleighs jingled back and forth on the statehouse lawn. But the previous years had not been so festive.

Kunin lost her first try for governor in 1982, when she ran against a popular incumbent. Undeterred by the loss, Kunin mounted a second campaign in 1984, this time against the state attorney general. While she had already served as lieutenant governor, voters worried that she was less experienced than her male opponent—a handicap she says is often part of being a woman in the political game.

Nevertheless, Kunin was able to display her qualifications successfully to the voters in 1984. One Vermont newspaper called her opponent "a candidate primarily of image," while Kunin was characterized as "a candidate primarily of substance and experience."

In her second gubernatorial campaign, Kunin also received significant assistance from female supporters that helped push her to the top. *National NOW Times* saw Kunin's victory as a win for feminist women.

> The Kunin election is distinct as a feminist victory in many ways. She is a feminist as were her campaign manager, fund raiser, scheduler and many of the hundreds of others who contributed to her victory. Kunin's donor base, at all levels of contribution, was 50% female. Much of the $200,000 she raised in out-of-state contributions came from feminist organizations and from events sponsored and attended by feminists.

Kunin's background in politics began not with women's issues, but with environmental concerns. A journalist and college teacher, Kunin joined other citizens working for a strong state environmental protection law in the 1960s. This experience led her to make a successful bid for a seat in the state legislature, where she worked for a land-use bill and a bottle ban. As a legislator, she was appointed chair of the House Appropriations Committee. In that position, she held the line on state spending and was able to keep property taxes down.

Many of those who supported Kunin's second try for governor did so on the basis of her vision for the future. Some of her various concerns, aside from protecting the environment, include strengthening Vermont's educational system, providing adequate child care for working parents, and working for a nuclear freeze. While such issues tend to be labeled "women's issues," the governor believes that many men are equally concerned.

The governor says that women who want to hold office must be able to take a stand. They must be willing to lead, to put their ideas and values on the line. Doing so may make them unpopular with some of their constituents.

> You have to build your credentials as a candidate, not just as a woman. You also have to be willing to exercise power. We've been educated to be mothers, peacemakers, but we must learn that we can't please everybody.

HOUSE SPEAKER VERA KATZ: GATHERING SUPPORT FOR ISSUES

Legislative leaders know that you can't please everyone. But their business is trying to win cooperation among different factions and rallying support for their programs. During the six months of the Sixty-third Session of the Oregon Legislative Assembly, two women put in especially long, complex days, working on one issue after another. Vera Katz presided over the House of Representatives; Shirley Gold was House majority leader. Some of their objectives were the same, but their styles were very different.

As House Speaker, Vera Katz was in the catbird seat. All important communication passed through her. All important business received her input. It took 101 ballots of the Democratic caucus for Katz to defeat the last of the male challengers for the top job. But when she won approval, she had no trouble assuming leadership. Unlike the previous Speaker, who let legislators choose their own committee chairs, Katz seized the opportunity to appoint her choices to these key positions, which immediately established her authority.

In regular business, it was she who approved the daily calendar; she was at the podium when the legislature convened. But much of her work was outside public view. At seven each morning she conferred with legislative leaders. From then on she dealt with a nonstop run of issues and decisions, pausing only to make a quick phone call or to leave the capitol to make a speech to an outside group. With luck, the day's business was finished by ten at night. At five she was often up again, working on a new speech or a sticky problem.

While Katz looked to committee chairs to target legislative priorities, her job was to help set direction and to create support for the legislative program. This meant getting representatives to cooperate with each other, and getting the public to approve of their overall goals.

Katz frequently talked to groups outside the legislature, showing one of the qualities that propelled her into leadership—strong communication skills. As a speaker, she adjusts her tone to the audience, shows a great command of her subject, and speaks to audience members as though they share with her an inside relationship. She can take a complex situation and put it into language an audience can follow.

On a typical day, Katz talked to Democratic precinct workers visiting the capitol. She was quiet, but forthright, talking without notes. "Traditionally Ds [the Democrats] don't talk about economic development. Mistake. We've got to talk about it," she told the party people. She also counseled them not to be divisive, not to "rail at each other, as Ds." The party people represent the grass roots, and Katz would like to have their approval. She is aware of her aura as a "city person," being from Portland and coming to the legislature from activist politics. The group were mostly small-town folk, who see politics from a different perspective.

The same day at a luncheon, Katz's audience was bipartisan and her style was more dramatic. The subject was money, and she was lobbying the Salem City Club for support for a new tax proposal. She reminded her listeners that some of the tax relief they received in the past causes trouble in the present. She gave them an oral quiz, to surprise them with how well Oregon has kept the lid on spending levels compared to the federal government. Then she hit them with a commonsense argument about tax reform. While she had a written speech, she scarcely used it. Her style was fast, breezy, and funny.

> In 1979 we had a lot of money. We decided to give it back to you. Anything that moved got seventy-five dollars. That was your income tax rebate, remember? The dumbest thing that we have ever done. The next dumbest thing was to say, Yeah, the state feels sorry for you and we're going to pay your property taxes!

Katz went on to explain how property tax relief is really paid for by increased income tax. "What looked like 30 percent relief is actually 13 percent! It doesn't make sense to take money out of one pocket and put it in another," she said. What she wanted from the audience was their backing for measures needed to reshuffle state taxes. Income taxes, property taxes, and a proposed sales tax would all be affected. She implored the audience to "stay open to the debate."

Back in the capitol, Katz continued one meeting after another with various legislators, including Senate President John Kitzhaber. Both leaders came into politics as activists in the early 1970s. Both have pictures of Robert Kennedy on their office walls. Conversation between the two is intricate

Vera Katz presides over Oregon's Legislative Assembly with authority and enthusiasm.

and fast-moving. Their legislative history and common background leads to a kind of verbal shorthand which an outsider would find hard to follow.

Compatibility with peers is important in legislative politics. Besides frequent meetings with the Senate president—who is a Democrat—Katz often confers with the Republican minority leader. Together they decide how to handle debates on legislation, whose names should go on particular bills, and such things as how to improve the legislature's credibility with the public. The previous session was heavily criticized for its infighting and failure to come up with some necessary measures. The leaders were glad to see an opinion poll that said their work on the Sixty-third Session had helped change the public's view.

Being criticized, misquoted, and misunderstood is part of the territory in public life. When Vera Katz spoke to the City Club, she was applauded and several audience members told her aide, "She's dynamite!" But on the way out of the meeting, Katz was stopped by three members of a powerful lobby who were not thrilled with her remarks. They made it clear they would oppose her objectives, and also quoted her in a way she said was false. But being challenged just seemed to fire the Speaker's spirit, rather than erode her confidence.

As a public figure, Katz creates a definite presence and stands for a definite point of view. Whether her work as the first woman in a tough job will lead to long-term success remains to be seen, she says. Katz told the Capitol Women's Political Caucus she hopes people will forget that she's unusual.

> People are not accustomed to a woman Speaker. It's a normalizing effect. My goal is for people to see it as natural. No disaster has occurred, there's been no occasion for people to say, "I told you so."

At the end of the session, the Senate president carried in a large bouquet of red roses and gave them to Katz at the House podium. The legislators laughed and applauded as Katz beamed and pounded the gavel, giving the last pronouncement, "If there is no more business, the House will adjourn *sine die*."

In the subsequent months, the press and the public would give their views on how well the body had done its job under its first woman Speaker.

MAJORITY LEADER SHIRLEY GOLD: BUILDING SUCCESSFUL LEGISLATION

Another woman chosen for leadership in the Sixty-third Session of the Oregon legislature was Representative Shirley Gold. A seasoned party worker and successful legislator, Gold was elected by Democratic representatives to manage the thirty-four-member Democratic caucus. Her job was to ride herd on all legislation proposed by Democratic House members, and to promote consensus among the members on which bills should get the most attention and how they should go about getting bills passed.

Gold's own record speaks for her ability to succeed. As chair of the Human Resources Committee in the previous session, Gold guided the study of seventy-five bills which were passed out of committee—all of which were approved by the House. This shows careful planning and conscious management. Bills do not wing their way through the legislative process on their own. "You do your best to work out the kinks before you put a bill to the test on the floor," Gold says.

A bill begins its path in the legislature when a sponsor brings it to the party caucus. Here the representative looks for allies and plans how to move the bill on its way—learning when to push and when to let it alone. Legislators can help each other succeed, but they can also disagree and block a bill's progress. Gold, who is a calm and thoughtful diplomat, was chosen to manage the caucus partly because of her background in negotiating different points of view. Her skill comes from experience.

As a teacher, union organizer, and mediator, Gold learned that pushing people and confronting them doesn't work. Different factions must feel they've been given a fair hearing in order for them to listen to other points of view.

Handling this process takes patience and the wisdom to sit

Shirley Gold, majority leader of the Oregon legislature, knows how to win cooperation from lawmakers with different points of view.

still while cooperation develops. Gold has these qualities, as well as a helpful belief system. She sees life as falling in cycles, rather than as a progress on a fixed line toward a perfect goal. If something is not attainable now, it may be possible to get it later, she believes. As majority leader, she maneuvered people into position to understand each other better, arranging meetings, passing information, and counseling legislators on the merits of particular bills.

Besides running the caucus office; conferring with a stream of representatives, lobbyists, and aides; chairing the Rules Committee; and testifying for specific pieces of legislation; Gold ran the caucus meetings. These are always behind closed doors, with only representatives and key aides allowed.

In a typical meeting, Gold might hear conflicting claims about a bill. When, for example, the meeting was about the state lottery, Gold forecast the discussion would be stormy. "Some legislators see it as a moral issue. They wish to judge how others will spend their money." Gold's own position on the lottery was not the point of the meeting. A negotiator has a different role.

Gold listened while different legislators talked about how much income the state could get from the lottery, how the money could go for economic development, how colleges and universities could benefit; and on the other hand, how a lottery might beguile innocent citizens and take their hard-earned money, how it could hook them on gambling. When one representative stormed out of the room, eyes blazing, Gold made a mental note to talk to him in the lunchroom and to see that he got a chance to vent his opinion the next time the caucus met.

> People who are good at this never put themselves into the controversy. They'll get the adversaries together and say, "Folks, we're going to have a bill, and you are going to come to agreement with one another on what's going to be in it." It can take a long time. Some of these major pieces of legislation can take months.

Even when the House was in its daily session, Gold was occupied with the business of the caucus. While one of her grown sons who was visiting sat at her desk in the House chamber one day, Gold worked the floor. Her task was to line up opposition to an open primary bill which would soon come up for a vote. She was looking for moderate and conservative support, as well as help from the liberals, to defeat the bill. Her staff had prepared a position paper which she could use to support the leadership point of view.

When working to promote a particular bill, Gold does not have time to go one-on-one to all the legislators in the caucus. She also may feel that someone else can do a better job of selling a particular bill. So part of her strategy is to dispatch certain legislators to build support within different circles. She tries to start a ripple effect that will spread.

But even if a bill gets the support it needs in the House and is sent on its way to the Senate, it can then be stopped in its tracks. When this happens Gold may summon one of the tricks she learned in past sessions. Recalling a bill that passed the House easily but was assigned to an unfriendly committee in the Senate, Gold says that "gutting and stuffing" saved it.

What Gold and her allies did was to take a Senate bill that was in their House committee—a bill that related to the same kind of issue—and delete the contents of the bill. Then they amended the bill by adding their own content (the content of the bill that was being held up in the Senate). The old content which had been deleted became a new bill, now sponsored by House members, and so everything was saved. "It's like playing chess," Gold says. "It's a game of removing obstacles." These tactics of gutting and stuffing can only be used sparingly, however.

The overall objective of the legislative session is to achieve the work it sets out to do at the beginning. During the Sixty-third Session, Gold defined as priorities as a tax relief measure, a streamlined budget, necessary revenue bills, and bills relating to a statewide water policy, economic development, and legislative reform. As majority leader, she could take a good deal of the credit for progress toward these goals.

In any case, sitting on the sidelines does not become Gold, who has long been active in political and community affairs.

Rather than sit back and complain that things aren't getting done the way I think they should be done, I somehow seek to be in the center of things—to get in there and try to be a part of accomplishing whatever can be done. If somehow it doesn't work out the way I thought it should, at least I can't blame myself for not trying.

ATTORNEY GENERAL
ARLENE VIOLET:
LOOKING AFTER
THE PUBLIC INTEREST

Arlene Violet, attorney general of Rhode Island, traces her political activism to her upbringing. She was raised in a family for whom public service was a way of life. Her father, a gas station owner and Republican alderman in Providence, regularly gave food and money to the poor. The nuns where she went to school also influenced her. The Sisters of Mercy, in long black habits, would go into the neighborhood after class "to shake down the merchants to make them donate meat and bread to the poor."

The nuns' example was striking to Violet. In those days women in such religious orders were very secluded. They were expected to stay out of sight, not confront people in ordinary life.

When Violet grew up, she joined the Sisters of Mercy, becoming an inner-city teacher, living and working in Providence's poorest neighborhoods. But her concern about some of the people's toughest problems eventually led her out of teaching and into law school. As an attorney, she chose to work as a trial lawyer defending the elderly, the handicapped, and consumer and environmental groups. Running for attorney general was a "natural transition," she said, because the job offered the chance to use the law to help even more people.

Deciding to run for office was "a very personal and painful" decision. As a nun, she was forbidden to seek office by the bishop of Providence, under directions from the Vatican. At first, Violet thought she could resign from her religious order, run for office, and if elected, serve, and later return to the order. But she was told that if she resigned, she could not return. Violet finally concluded that "It's important to be a Sister of Mercy in reality even if you may have to forfeit being one in name."

When she was elected in 1984, receiving 51 percent of the vote and unseating the third-term incumbent, Violet told the press that her choice hadn't been easy: "This race has been so symbolic of my entire life. I have always had to struggle before I got to victory."

Victory meant taking the reins as chief legal officer in Rhode Island. The attorney general's power is considerable. Some of the services and responsibilities of the AG's office are representing the state in all civil and criminal cases before state and federal courts, enforcing state and federal antitrust laws, giving opinions to the governor and other officials on proposed courses of action, investigating organized crime and public corruption, and providing consumer protection and information services.

Violet says it was "important to set the tone" when taking office. Her no-nonsense style of energy, concentration, and precision earned her the nickname "the General." As head of the state's chief prosecuting office, Violet could use her power to put resources on specific problem areas. She decided to make street crime—which plagues the elderly and the poor—her priority.

Violet's decision to attack street crime meant opening up investigations into charges of political corruption. Violet doesn't doubt that it exists. Rhode Island's capital, Providence, has long been alleged to be a center for organized crime in New England. And there can be no organized crime without payoffs to officials.

Violet also wants to ensure speedy trials for high-trauma crimes such as assaults on the elderly and rape. "If you don't try them right away, you can kiss them goodbye," she says of cases involving these kinds of violence.

Violet hopes to do an exceptional job, not only for the issues involved, but also for the sake of other women. "I don't want to foreclose other talented women from having this position," she said. "I just want to make sure I keep the position open for them."

For Violet, public service and politics go hand in hand. "I grew up with that sense that you are here to serve people. I consider that the best tradition of politics."

★ 6 ★

IN THE HALLS
OF CONGRESS

It has often been said that it is a liability for a candidate to be a woman. But studies of women's campaigns for Congress have shown this assertion to be somewhat of a myth. The fact is, women rate more positively than men on seven of ten characteristics that are important to voters. According to a study by the National Women's Political Caucus of voter perceptions, women rate higher than men on caring, being effective, having strong opinions, having new ideas, fighting for their beliefs, understanding the needs of the voters, and speaking directly to the point.

Women rate as well as men on two other characteristics: having leadership qualities and the ability to build a feeling of confidence. The one characteristic on which women rate lower than men is the ability to handle a crisis. This negative stereotype plagued Geraldine Ferraro during her run for the vice presidency.

But Ferraro's candidacy may have done much to dispel that negative stereotype. After the election, more than one out of four voters told interviewers that they would be more likely to support women in the future. And 35 percent of first-time voters said they would be more likely to support women in the future.

A study of the 1984 election results, commissioned by the National Women's Political Caucus, has concluded: "There is very definitely a greater propensity among voters to support a woman running for public office today than we would have found before the Ferraro candidacy. The scene has been set for a much greater level of participation of women in the very near future."

CLASS OF '84

Compared with men, women in Congress so far have been a distinct minority. New York State claims the record for having sent the most women to Congress—a total of twelve, all to the House of Representatives. Both Illinois and California have sent eight women to the House, Connecticut and New Jersey each have sent five, and Maryland has sent six. Four states—Alabama, Louisiana, Nebraska, and South Dakota—have been represented twice by women in the Senate. Three states—Maine, Kansas, and Florida—have been represented once by women in the Senate. Ten states have never sent a woman to either the House or the Senate.

More women were candidates in the congressional elections of 1984 than in any previous election. There were 75 women nominated for office by the major parties, including 39 Republicans and 36 Democrats. Of those 75 women, 10 ran for Senate seats—twice the previous record of 5. The remaining 65 ran for seats in the House—ten more than the previous high of 55.

Not all of the women who ran for Congress were winners, of course. But the very fact that more women ran than ever before lends support to a hopeful conclusion: women are becoming more credible as candidates and officeholders in the eyes of party leaders and voters alike.

Of the ten women who ran for the Senate in 1984, only one was elected. That was Nancy Landon Kassebaum, Republican of Kansas. As an incumbent running for reelection, Kassebaum enjoyed all the advantages that incumbents traditionally enjoy, including greater familiarity with the voters and better media coverage. Kassebaum's only female colleague in the Senate, Paula Hawkins, Republican of Florida, faced reelection in 1986.

Of the 65 women who ran for seats in the House of Representatives, 23 were elected. Most of them were incumbents, too. As a result of the 1984 elections, 23 women were seated in the House of Representatives in the Ninety-ninth Congress (1985–87), including 12 Democrats and 11 Republicans.

The Democrats in the House were Corinne (Lindy) Boggs, Louisiana; Barbara Boxer, California; Sala Burton, California; Beverly Byron, Maryland; Cardiss Collins, Illinois; Marcy Kaptur, Ohio; Barbara Bailey Kennelly, Connecticut; Marilyn Lloyd, Tennessee; Cathy Long, Louisiana; Barbara Mikulski, Maryland; Mary Rose Oakar, Ohio; and Patricia Schroeder, Colorado.

The Republicans were Helen Delich Bentley, Maryland; Bobbi Fiedler, California; Marjorie Holt, Maryland; Nancy Johnson, Connecticut; Lynn Martin, Illinois; Jan Meyers, Kansas; Margaret Roukema, New Jersey; Claudine Schneider, Rhode Island; Virginia Smith, Nebraska; Olympia Snowe, Maine; and Barbara Vucanovich, Nevada.

POWER IN CONGRESS

Women in Congress have tended to be seen as less powerful than men because few of them have won assignments on committees that their male colleagues perceive as most important. Sitting on a judiciary or agriculture committee may best serve a congresswoman's constituents, but it will not earn her great fame or prestige.

Certain committees are credited with being more important or powerful than others; that is, they have a greater say on certain kinds of legislation and they attract greater public attention. For that reason, members have traditionally competed for assignments to those committees. In the House, members compete for places on Appropriations, Rules, and Ways and Means. In the Senate, the most desirable committee assignments are Appropriations, Finance, Foreign Relations, and Armed Services.

Until recent times, committee assignments were made exclusively on the basis of seniority, on the principle, as one Speaker of the House put it, of "let them wait." While seniority remains the single most important consideration, congressional leaders today take other factors into account as they make committee assignments. These other considerations include the member's party standing ("Is she a 'regular' or a maverick?"); her geographical origin ("Do we need that area represented?"); and, finally, her interests and expertise.

Committee chairs are truly powerful members of Congress. They schedule meetings and decide what bills will be taken up. They often control the appointment of subcommittee chairs, and the hiring and firing of the committee staff. In some cases a committee chair can pigeonhole a bill simply by refusing to hold hearings. Traditionally, the chair of a committee is the committee member from the majority party in Congress with the longest record of uninterrupted service.

Seven women have chaired congressional committees— Senator Hattie Caraway, Democrat of Arkansas; and Representatives Martha Griffiths, Democrat of Minnesota; Mae Nolan, Republican of California; Mary Norton, Democrat of New Jersey; Caroline O'Day, Democrat of New York; Edith Rogers, Republican of Massachusetts; and Leonor Sullivan, Democrat of Missouri. No woman has ever been Speaker of the House or majority or minority leader of either the House or Senate.

Today Republican senator Nancy Kassebaum holds what are considered impressive committee assignments. The daughter of Alf Landon, onetime governor of Kansas and Republican candidate for president in 1936, Kassebaum has a proud heritage. But when she ran for the Senate in 1978, she had little officeholding experience, having served only on a local school board. Nevertheless, she won an upset victory. She was reelected easily in 1984.

Kassebaum's committee assignments are Commerce, Foreign Relations, and Budget. On Foreign Relations, she is in a position to have an impact on American foreign policy. Less hawkish than her Republican Senate colleagues, she favors negotiated settlements over military solutions. She led the team that monitored El Salvador's elections in 1984. As chair of the Africa subcommittee, she works to maintain aid to black African countries and to isolate South Africa, because of its policy of racial separation known as "apartheid." Kassebaum has the qualities that enable her to become a Senate insider. The respected *Almanac of American Politics* says of her, "She is one who appreciates arguments on both sides of an issue

*Senator Nancy Kassebaum, with her colleagues,
Representative John Murtha, D-Pa. (left) and
Representative Robert Livingston, R-La.,
conducted a news conference in El Salvador during
her mission as head of the U.S. team monitoring
elections in that country.*

. . . and she is respected in the Senate for learning her job quietly rather than in the full glare of publicity."

A DAY
IN THE LIFE

A day in the life of a member of Congress always begins early and often continues well into the night. Members from large states have more constituents to service than members from small states, and senior members are likely to be more heavily involved in committee work than junior members. But the typical day of a member of Congress is made up of more or less the same kinds of activities.

Patricia Schroeder, the representative from Colorado's first congressional district (Denver), has sat in the House of Representatives since 1973. One day in early 1986, her schedule included a meeting of the Democratic Caucus on the budget; closed hearings of the Armed Services Committee on the B-1 bomber program; luncheon with a Jewish women's organization, where she talked about women's issues; a meeting with her staff, followed by an hour for phone calls and correspondence; a roll call vote on the floor of the House; meetings with visiting constituents, including wheat growers, service station dealers, and students; a fund-raiser for a colleague on Congress at a nearby hotel; and a black tie dinner at the Canadian embassy.

As travel has become easier, meetings with constituents take up more and more of a member's time. "I represent a district that's two thousand miles away," says Schroeder, "so obviously, when they come in, you have to be attentive. Often these visits deal with law-making in a very general sense, 'We like this law,' 'We don't like that law,' 'Vote for this,' or 'Don't vote for that.' "

A member is expected to spend a great deal of time in her district, even if it happens to be two or three thousand miles distant. Members are reimbursed for one trip to their district each month, but Schroeder spends many weekends in Denver, flying out on the "red-eye" express on Thursday or Friday evening, and returning to Washington on the red-eye on Sunday night. "There are days when you think that you're never, ever going to land again," Schroeder says.

In Denver Schroeder's schedule is much the same as it is in Washington, with problems to hear and resolve, fences to mend, remarks to make, and her son's performance in a school play to catch. "I try to be out and around as much as I can, Schroeder says, "because there are a lot of people who would like to talk with you, but are just a little hesitant to make an appointment." In Denver, as in Washington, time is her biggest problem. "I usually get home at two in the morning," she says, "and I'm up again by 6:30 for a breakfast or some such event."

Schroeder is not alone in viewing constituent services as one of her most important duties. One study of the work that members do revealed that they spend as much as 28 percent of their time servicing their constituents. That task usually involves cutting through red tape to get something that a constituent is entitled to.

A "SAFE SEAT"

Over the years, Schroeder and her constituents have built up a strong rapport, seeing eye-to-eye on most important issues. Only one in four of Denver's households today includes children; less than half include a married couple. Its voters include a large number of young singles and older residents. Denver's young whites, Mexican-Americans, and blacks tend to be liberal on both economic and social issues. Because Schroeder is so well attuned to those attitudes, her district has become safer for her with each election.

Born in 1940 in Portland, Oregon, Schroeder received her B.S. degree from the University of Minnesota in 1961, and her law degree from Harvard in 1964. At Harvard Law School, she was a classmate of Elizabeth Holzman, who would also sit in Congress, and Elizabeth Dole, who would serve as the secretary of transportation. After marrying and settling in Denver, Schroeder practiced law for a while, and taught law at the University of Denver and other local colleges.

In her first campaign for Congress, Schroeder ran on an

As a member of the House Armed Services Committee,
Representative Patricia Schroeder has sometimes supported
causes that are not popular with others on the committee.
In 1980, for example, she opposed President Carter's call
for resumption of draft registration.

anti–Vietnam War, proenvironment platform that led to victory in an upset election. For years after her election, conservatives spent large sums of money trying to unseat her, but by 1982 they had given up. In 1984 not even the Republican landslide accompanying Ronald Reagan's reelection was enough to stop her from winning her seventh term in the House.

With fifteen years' experience in the House, Schroeder has gained seniority and won increasing clout. In her freshman term, she won a seat on the Armed Services Committee over the heated objections of its chairman, F. Edward Hebert, who deplored the idea of having an anti–Vietnam War woman on the committee. "He did his best to make me uncomfortable," she recalls, "but I wasn't going to let him embarrass me off the committee." By working hard, and by not abandoning her positions, Schroeder won grudging respect from her colleagues on Armed Services.

After fifteen years of service on Armed Services, she is the ninth-ranking Democrat on a committee of forty. She has almost reached the level that would, by seniority, entitle her to be named subcommittee chair. Her special concerns as a committee member have included personnel matters such as pensions, as well as regulations affecting women in the armed forces.

Schroeder has worked to get chemical weaponry out of the Rocky Mountains Arsenal near Denver. She has opposed most controversial weapons systems, such as the MX missile. Such views are popular with her constituents but not with her colleagues on the Armed Services Committee, most of whom favor high defense spending and seldom question Pentagon recommendations. Even so, Schroeder's views generally find support on the floor of the House, where she is always well enough prepared to gain a hearing from colleagues, if not to win them over.

As a member of the Judiciary Committee, Schroeder can be counted on to vote for the Equal Rights Amendment and against an antiabortion amendment to the Constitution. As chair of a Post Office and Civil Service subcommittee, she is a champion of federal workers. As one of the federal government's regional centers, Denver has a large number of well-organized federal employees.

The most important ingredient of a successful career in politics, says Schroeder, is liking people. "If you don't love people, you're in real trouble. This is a society where we tend to be more patient with machinery than we are with each other. It's always amazing to me how we become technology junkies. I wish we became more human junkies, liking each other much more."

MAXIMIZING THE POWER OF WOMEN

Besides serving as lawmakers for the people and advocates for their constituents, some women in Congress take a special interest in women's issues, believing that they have a special responsibility to do so. In their commitment to feminist objectives, women in Congress range from lukewarm to enthusiastic, yet women—and men—of many political persuasions operate harmoniously in the Congressional Caucus for Women's Issues.

A caucus is a group of members who share certain goals and who meet privately to agree on a common strategy for achieving those goals. More than seventy caucus groups of varying makeups and sizes operate in the House and the Senate. In 1977 women in Congress formed the Congressional Women's Caucus to promote legislation that improves the condition of women, and to monitor the operation of federal programs dealing with women.

At first, membership in the caucus was limited to women. But in 1981 it changed its name to the Congressional Caucus for Women's Issues and admitted male members of Congress as well. At the same time, the caucus established the Women's Research and Education Institute to provide research, education and technical support.

Today fifteen of the twenty-three women in Congress belong to the caucus. One hundred and ten of the 512 male members of Congress also belong. Although the caucus is bipartisan, its membership is heavily Democratic. Five of the fifteen women who belong, and ten of the 110 men, are Republican. The rest are Democrats. The executive committee of the caucus is cochaired by Representatives Pat Schroeder, Democrat of Colorado, and Olympia Snowe, Republican of Maine.

COEXISTENCE
ON THE CAUCUS

In many ways, Snowe is at the opposite end of the ideological spectrum from Schroeder. Born in 1947 in Augusta, Maine, she received her B.A. from the University of Maine in 1969 and entered state politics soon after. In 1973 she was elected to Maine's House of Representatives, where she served until 1976. In that year she ran for and was elected to the state Senate, where she served until 1978. She then ran a successful race for a seat in the U.S. House of Representatives, where she is serving her fourth term.

Snowe has been described as "a visceral, partisan Repub lican." As a member of the Foreign Affairs Committee, she concentrates her committee work on foreign policy and defense issues, on which she is cautiously conservative. Yet her position on women's issues brands her as a moderate and divides her from President Reagan.

Liberals and conservatives can coexist in the women's caucus, Snowe told a *New York Times* reporter, "because on social issues, on women's issues, we all tend to be in the center." The strategic challenge for the caucus, Snowe says, is "to find common ground for common action." The caucus has to be careful to avoid issues that divide its members.

NIBBLING AWAY

Another challenge for members of the caucus is to keep their agenda visible in the minds of their colleagues, letting them know subtly that support for their own projects is at stake. "It's not easy," says Snowe; "you just have to keep nibbling away. There are so many issues that members of Congress are involved in or concentrating on in a general session that it's a mark of success when you can even draw attention to a specific issue."

Caucus meetings are usually strategy sessions. Once the members have agreed on objectives, they work out a legislative strategy for achieving them. "We sit down and develop strategies and priorities to get as many of the statutes through Congress as possible," Snowe says. "We've tried to develop a network among ourselves. We divide up the committees in question, we have vote counters, Democrats lobby Democrats, Republicans lobby Republicans, and we try to keep everyone abreast of when they should be on the floor fighting for votes."

The caucus publicizes its agenda through *Update*, a monthly newsletter that goes to about 4,500 people. Members of the caucus also ask to testify before congressional committees that have scheduled hearings on matters that concern the caucus. In 1984, as members of the House filed onto the floor to vote on two child-care measures, they found a member of the caucus stationed at each door of the chamber with handouts and a message: "Vote yes." The measure passed.

As the first session of the Ninety-ninth Congress ended in December 1985, the caucus and its allies scored important victories in Congress. They passed a law that earmarks a new high of $1.56 billion for the Special Supplemental Food Program for Women, Infants, and Children. They also won funding for two other programs they consider very important—family violence prevention and child care. But they were still fighting for the reauthorization of funds of child nutrition programs, and for other important objectives.

At no time since the Congressional Caucus for Women's Issues was formed have social welfare programs been so threatened as they are today. In the Reagan years, those who favor the expansion of such programs have become a minority. And even programs that enjoy broad support—such as the school lunch program—have been threatened by budget cutters. "It's in times like these," says cochair Snowe, "that the caucus becomes absolutely indispensable."

★ 7 ★

IN THE EXECUTIVE
AND
JUDICIAL BRANCHES

No woman yet has been elected president or vice president of
the United States, but women have played an increasingly
important role in the presidency ever since Frances Perkins
served in the Cabinet of President Franklin D. Roosevelt.

The presidency includes not only the president, but all
those groups and individuals on whom the president depends
to perform the duties of chief executive, commander in chief,
and party leader. In ever-widening circles, those groups and
individuals include the following:

The White House staff, which is made up of the president's
immediate deputies and assistants;

The Executive Office of the President, whose half dozen
key agencies, such as the National Security Council, serve the
president in policy making;

The vice president, who succeeds the president in case of
death or disability; and

The Cabinet, which includes the heads of the thirteen
departments that make up the executive branch of the federal
government—the secretaries of the Departments of Agriculture, Commerce, Defense, Education, Energy, Health and
Human Services, Housing and Urban Development, the In-
terior, Labor, State, Transportation, and Treasury; and the
attorney general, who heads the Department of Justice.

High posts within each of these bodies are appointive,
rather than elective. In recent years, larger percentages of these
appointments have been going to women. But more recently,

there have been complaints of slippage. In 1984, 17.5 percent of what *Congressional Quarterly* calls major appointments went to women. In 1985 the figure was 15.5 percent. More significant is the fact that the inner circles of power are nearly devoid of women.

WHITE HOUSE INSIDERS

A creation of modern times, the White House staff grew larger and more powerful as the duties of the president became more numerous and complex. Members of the White House staff perform countless tasks that are essential to presidential decision-making and control.

Some of them act as gatekeepers and guardians of the president's time, planning the daily schedule and deciding who will receive appointments. Others serve as the president's links with the various departments of government, the Congress, the party, and the public. Still others advise the president on policy matters, such as appropriate positions on arms control, farm relief, and so on. There are advisers on political questions, such as which candidate to support in a state or local primary. There are speechwriters and press officers who speak in the president's behalf to the press.

Day-by-day proximity to the president gives members of the White House staff enormous influence, including the opportunity to shape the chief executive's view of the world, priorities, and actions. For that reason, feminists, like other groups, have tried to influence appointments to both of these groups. With "friends at court," a group can command the attention and influence the decisions of the president.

In late 1985, members of the White House staff told Jane Meyer, a reporter for *The Wall Street Journal* that women had lost ground in the White House. For the first time since 1977, they said, no woman at the White House was of high enough rank to attend the important daily senior staff meetings or report directly to the president. What was once the top-ranking White House post held by a woman—head of public liaison—had been bumped down a notch in status. Only three second-level posts were held by women, and only one of those was considered to be a policy post.

The situation was reported to be no better in the Executive Office of the President. The Executive Office includes such key agencies as the Office of Management and Budget (OMB), which prepares the federal budget; the Council of Economic Advisers (CEA), which gives advice on economic policy; and the National Security Council (NSC), which advises the president on foreign policy and defense issues, and oversees crisis management from the situation room in the basement of the White House. Some observers believe that women were appointed to the Reagan administration simply as window dressing. With reelection behind him, they say, President Reagan is less concerned about the gender gap, and showcasing is over. During his first administration, for example, Jeane Kirkpatrick, as ambassador to the United Nations, was a member of the National Security Council. Since Kirkpatrick's departure in 1984, no woman has regularly attended NSC meetings, or held a high post in any agency of the Executive Office.

According to Kirkpatrick, "Sexism is alive in the White House." She has told reporters of the campaign by male colleagues to keep her ambitions in check. "One of them said that I was too temperamental to hold a higher office. What do they mean—too temperamental once a month?" Kirkpatrick told reporter Jane Meyer of seeing a mouse in the situation room, while attending a meeting of the NSC. "I thought to myself," she said, "that the mouse was no more surprising a creature to see in the situation room than I. I don't know if I'm the only woman who has ever sat around the table in the situation room. I know I'm the only one in this administration." Columnist Ellen Goodman writes, "Chief of staff Donald Regan has gone back to the white male talent agency for his central casting."

THE CABINET: A TALE
OF TWO SECRETARIES

On the surface, at least, women have made stronger inroads in the Reagan Cabinet than on the White House staff or in Executive Office positions. President Reagan appointed a woman, Jeane Kirkpatrick, ambassador to the United Nations, in his first term in office. And he named two women—Elizabeth Hanford Dole and Margaret Heckler—to his Cabinet, the seventh and eighth women, respectively, to administer executive departments.

In many ways, the position of a Cabinet secretary is difficult. While the Constitution designates the members of the Cabinet as advisers to the president, they can also be adversaries. Their loyalty extends downward to their own departments, as well as upward to the president. After a while, they tend to adopt the parochial view of their departments, competing with other Cabinet members for bigger budgets and presidential favor. Sometimes secretaries have close ties with powerful members of Congress or interest groups. These relationships give them power independent of the president. For reasons such as these, Charles G. Dawes, vice president during the administration of President Calvin Coolidge, concluded, "The members of the Cabinet are a President's natural enemies."

To survive, a Cabinet member needs political astuteness, rather than expertise in a given field. Generally, the administration makes the basic decisions, trying to keep the secretaries inside the corral. The most basic challenge for a secretary is to exert real power. Otherwise she or he ends up looking like a mere messenger.

Elizabeth Hanford Dole:
Secretary of Transportation

In 1982 Elizabeth Hanford Dole was chosen to head the massive U.S. Department of Transportation (DOT), with its thousands of employees dispersed from coast to coast and at sea. Loosely grouped under DOT are several major agencies, including the United States Coast Guard, the Federal Aviation Administration, and the Federal Highway Administration.

Among the major challenges facing Dole when she took over was the rehabilitation of the air traffic control system, which was left in shambles after a strike by controllers in 1981. By 1985 she had succeeded in building up the personnel of that system to prestrike levels, although critics have charged that she has dragged her feet, and that there are still too few controllers. Dole also has been less than successful in her efforts to steer a proposed trucking deregulation bill past White

House aides, who worry about the impact on Reagan's allies in the Teamsters union.

Dole chalked up a victory when she persuaded the administration to make auto safety a central concern. Soon after taking office, the administration rescinded a 1977 rule that required either airbags or automatic seat belts in cars beginning in 1982. But the Supreme Court declared that move illegal. In an effort to compromise, Dole devised a plan to force auto makers to install passive restraints starting on September 1, 1989, unless states accounting for two-thirds of the population adopt strict seat-belt laws by April 1, 1989.

So far, thirteen states have done so, although it's not clear that Dole regards the laws as tough enough "I was amazed she could sell that to the administration," said Senate Commerce Committee Chair John C. Danforth, Republican of Missouri, who supports stiffer measures. Yet, at the same time, Dole has alienated consumer groups, one of which has stated, "Dole caved in to the auto companies."

All of Dole's other problems look small next to her biggest undertaking—the sale of the government's controlling interest in Consolidated Rail Corporation (CONRAIL), the big Northeast freight carrier. The administration wanted to complete the sale before the 1984 election, aiming to dramatize its goal of privatization. Failing to persuade Congress to adopt her plan, Dole could not meet her deadline.

Dole wants to sell CONRAIL to a competing railroad, Norfolk Southern Corporation. But a bipartisan group of lawmakers, worried about possible job losses and reduced freight competition, favors another option. Dole has a good chance of getting her proposal through the Senate, but there is stronger opposition to her plan in the House. Still Dole is pushing, saying, "I'm a great believer that the federal government should not be running railroads."

Shrewd political instincts and good timing landed Dole her job at DOT. She actively lobbied for the job, and she got it because the chemistry was right. At the time, the White House sought to woo women voters with a female Cabinet appointment, and Dole had the credentials and the experience.

For Dole the appointment was one more achievement in a climb to power that began twenty years before. She had

At a news conference, Transportation Secretary
Elizabeth Dole hands a model train to Bob Claytor,
chairman of Norfolk Southern Corporation.

decided on a career in government as a high school student in North Carolina. She graduated from Duke University, where she was elected both May Queen and Phi Beta Kappa. In 1960 she earned a master's degree at Harvard, and entered Harvard Law School, one of twenty-five women in a class of more than five hundred.

From law school, Dole went to work as a staff assistant to the assistant secretary for education in the Department of Health, Education, and Welfare. She left government briefly to try private law practice, but at President Richard Nixon's request, returned to government as executive director of the President's Committee for Consumer Interests.

Dole moved on to the U.S. Office of Consumer Affairs, headed by Virginia H. Knauer. Knauer says of her former deputy, "Elizabeth proved so outstanding that I asked her to be my deputy, jumping her over everyone else. She is intellectually brilliant, but she also has pragmatic political sense, and you need that in the White House."

In 1973 Dole's climb to the top got steeper. After her nomination to one of five seats on the Federal Trade Commission (FTC), she encountered her first opposition. The spot had been earmarked for a strong consumer advocate, and the Senate Commerce Committee chair felt she was too closely linked with the White House consumer office, which was not activist enough to suit the committee.

Because of her work at the White House, Dole knew many key people in the consumer field. With their support, she knew she could win the FTC seat. On the weekend after her nomination, she took a plane to a major consumer conference, where she got an impressive list of supporters. She went after the job and got it. Once there, she proved herself a powerful defender of consumers. Former FTC staffers describe her as independent, fair-minded, and hardworking. She personally promoted enforcement of the Equal Credit Opportunity Act of 1975, which prohibits discrimination by creditors on the basis of sex or marital status.

It was in 1975 that Elizabeth Hanford married Senator Robert Dole, Republican of Kansas, the majority leader of the Senate, a onetime vice presidential candidate, and contender for the presidential nomination in 1988. Described as "the power couple," the Doles refused to cover up political differences between themselves. A friend has said, "Neither of them will back off from a good fight." In 1977, Elizabeth supported the creation of a strong consumer advocacy agency, and Robert opposed it. Instead of avoiding the issue, the Doles staged a debate. In addition to open debate, the Doles "compartmentalize" information that they decide not to discuss with each other.

In 1980 Dole served on the White House staff as the president's liaison with interest groups. She had the often delicate task of explaining White House policy to labor, business, ethnic, and other groups, and conveying their positions to the president. While she was never part of the all-male inner circle, she gained their respect by being a team player. Her support for the Equal Rights Amendment and other feminist objectives was well known. But she was, in the words of a reporter for *Time*, "a loyal soldier who would lock her smile on automatic pilot to lobby for Reagan's conservative agenda, despite her own, more moderate political views."

In Dole, women's groups felt that they had a friend in the White House. Kathy Wilson, chair of the National Women's Political Caucus, said, "Dole was the first person to get the White House going on women's issues. And that was as big a task as administering a cabinet agency."

Often mentioned as a prospective vice presidential candidate for the Republican party, Dole has got to compile a creditable record as secretary of transportation. While her record so far has been mixed, her reputation as a good administrator and savvy politician is untarnished. Hers has been a different experience altogether from that of Margaret Heckler.

Margaret Heckler:
Secretary of Health and Human Services
Not long before her abrupt resignation in 1985, Margaret Heckler suggested that "women in and near the White House are subject to double standards. There's far more tolerance of incompetent males than of women." The circumstances of Heckler's departure from the Cabinet tend to confirm her observation.

Heckler was appointed secretary of the Department of Health and Human Services (HHS) in 1982, after losing an election that ended sixteen years in the House of Representatives. She was the third woman to head HHS or its predecessors. For good reasons, she called her job "the hardest assignment in Washington." She ran a bureaucracy employing more than 145,000 and dispensing a budget of $276 billion—the third largest budget in the world after those of the United States and the Soviet Union. HHS administers Social Security, Medicare and Medicaid, Aid to Families with Dependent Children, health care programs, and research.

Heckler's appointment to HHS stunned conservative Republicans. They oppose many of the programs that HHS runs, and expect them to be eliminated. Heckler, a moderate Republican, supported some of those programs in the past, just as she supported ERA. Conservatives high in the Reagan administration—among them, a former deputy of Heckler's who was strongly opposed to her appointment and policies—were out to get her from the start.

Those who follow Heckler's career call her "tough" and "feisty," saying that she can take care of herself. A former associate has described how Heckler took on President Nixon at the 1972 Republication convention, insisting on the addition to the party platform of a new plank on day-care. She won, and the day-care plank was the only addition to the Nixon-dictated Republican party platform on which Nixon and all other Republican candidates ran that year.

Heckler was born Margaret Mary O'Shaughnessy in Flushing, Queens, New York, in 1931, the daughter of Irish immigrants. She got a taste of politics as an undergraduate at Albertus Magnus College in New Haven, when she was a successful candidate for speaker of the Connecticut Intercollegiate Student Legislature.

She attended Boston College Law School and graduated sixth in her class in 1956. Active in Boston politics for several years, she decided to run for Congress in 1966. She won in a stunning upset, defeating a popular former House Speaker in the Republican primary. She was reelected to each succeeding Congress until 1982, when she lost to a Democratic incumbent, Barney Frank, in a fiercely contested race to represent a reapportioned district regarded as one of the most liberal in the nation.

In the House of Representatives, Heckler skillfully walked a fine line between loyalty to the Republican party and responsiveness to her constituents, who were liberal and largely Democratic. Throughout her career, she had been an ardent advocate of women's rights and a strong supporter of ERA, as moderate Republicans had been for decades. A Catholic, she opposed abortion, but did not oppose the Supreme Court decision that legalized it, as well as policies providing for family planning assistance. In her final term in the House, she voted for only 40 percent of the measures proposed by President Reagan.

Given her record in Congress, it was inevitable that Heckler would find herself out of place in the Reagan administration. Politically, her job was to defend the fairness of the president's budget and tax policies in response to charges by the Democrats that the policies helped the rich and hurt the poor. As head of HHS, she toed the Reagan line. She had a standard response to questions dealing with conflicts of loyalties and party infighting: "I am the President's Secretary of Health and Human Services, and implementing his goals will be my priority."

Rather than forcefully confronting critics of administration policy, Heckler tried, with some success, to persuade elderly people, doctors, hospitals, and members of antipoverty groups that she was representing their interests within the administration. She supported tax credits for day-care and lobbied effectively to strengthen laws on child-support payments.

She encouraged additional research on Alzheimer's disease and obtained more money for the study of acquired immune deficiency syndrome, or AIDS. Her defenders praised her for reducing Medicare cost inflation, and her efforts to protect the poor and elderly against budget cutters.

Although Heckler was praised outside the administration for these and other accomplishments and initiatives, such issues were not viewed by the White House as major conservative goals. White House officials contended that Heckler was a weak administrator, at the same time conceding that it is not easy for anyone to control a department that runs such huge programs as Social Security, Medicare, and Medicaid.

But by all accounts, it was a clash of personalities between Heckler and White House chief of staff Donald T. Regan that finally led to her dismissal. Regan was said to be unsympathetic to feminism in general, and less than receptive to having women on the White House staff. Rumors of Heckler's dismissal began circulating not long after President Reagan's reelection in November 1984, but not until the following year did those rumors surface in the press. "Heckler Fights Effort to Oust Her from Post" read a *New York Times* headline in September 1985. In a series of leaks that angered the president and his chief of staff, White House aides confirmed that Chief of Staff Regan was determined to have Heckler dismissed, hoping to persuade the president to appoint her ambassador to Ireland. According to those unnamed individuals who talked to the press, Regan found Heckler abrasive, tending to challenge administration officials, including Regan.

As an example of that tendency, Regan said that Heckler once had stated that only the president, who appointed her, could remove her. Besides that, Regan complained of Heckler's lateness at Cabinet meetings, her lack of preparation and indecisiveness. Finally, he believed that Heckler was "disorganized." The last criticism focused on the large number of vacancies in her department. But Heckler said that the White House created the problem by rejecting several of her choices, or taking as long as eight months to approve them.

Heckler professed to be baffled by the move to oust her: "I cannot decipher the reason for it because there is no issue of substance dividing me from the White House. I have faithfully carried the President's portfolio." She later told a reporter for *U.S. News & World Report*: "Frankly, I was the victim of a long-term vendetta by one individual in the White House. It went on for years. So the well was poisoned. I was never given support by the team."

In an effort to keep her post, Heckler rounded up a few powerful figures to lend support, including conservative Republican senator Orrin Hatch, Republican senator Alan Simpson, and Senate Majority Leader Robert Dole. These men and others put in a good word for Heckler at the White House. Senator Hatch said that Heckler was doing "a terrific job." Hatch continued: "The campaign by the White House to denigrate Margaret has been pathetic and disgusting, and I am outraged by it." Heckler's adversaries in the White House saw her efforts to round up support as evidence of disloyalty to the administration.

Once the story of her impending dismissal had appeared in print, Heckler requested a meeting with the president. Aides to Heckler said she wanted to meet with the president alone because she wanted to know with certainty whether he was dissatisfied with her. If the president was dissatisfied, they said, she would resign, because she serves at his pleasure.

Regan wanted Heckler to meet with him, rather than the president, an administration official said. "Regan doesn't want a scene in the Oval Office. If she insists on seeing the President, Regan will insist on being in the room." In a forty-minute meeting with the president, Heckler was asked to become ambassador to Ireland, a job that the White House press secretary said "the president considers a promotion." Not long before, Heckler had described the Ireland post, which would reduce her salary, influence, and status in terms of protocol, as "a lovely position for someone else."

The day after their first meeting, President Reagan appeared before the press with Heckler at his side, announcing that she would accept the post of ambassador. The president told reporters her new position was a reward for her "fine job." He denied reports that she was being removed because he and senior White House aides were dissatisfied with her performance.

Heckler said she had accepted the ambassadorial post because "when the Great Communicator, our leader, the President of the United States, asks one to take on an assignment, it would be irresponsible for one who has served in public office for all these years of public service, to have said no." She said that she was "proud" of her record as secretary of health and human services and that she had been faithful to the president's philosophy. Asked if she were conservative enough, the president remarked, "You bet she is."

Heckler faced a dilemma that all Cabinet members face: that of proving herself loyal, while at the same time showing independence and will. She also came up against the double standard: the stricter standards to which women are held. When she turned to powerful allies to confront her enemies in the White House, she was accused of disloyalty. In the end, she lacked sufficient allies to make a difference. As a woman, she lacked the power network that men have built up over the years.

WOMEN ON
FEDERAL COURTS

The Supreme Court is the pinnacle of the American system of justice, but it is only one part of a decentralized system that also includes a network of federal courts, state and local courts, and the United States Department of Justice.

Immediately below the Supreme Court are the United States Courts of Appeals. Called "circuit courts," they hear appeals from lower federal courts. They have the final word on nearly every contested act of federal regulatory agencies. Below the circuit courts are the federal district courts, which are trial courts. In 1984 district judges made more than 300,000 criminal and civil case decisions, many of them affecting individuals more directly than decisions of the Supreme Court.

All federal judges are appointed by the president for life, subject to Senate approval. Between 1934, the year of Florence Ellinwood Allen's appointment, and 1977, only ten women had been named to the federal bench. During the Carter administration, however—partly because 152 new judgeships were created—41 women were named. Brooksley Landau, chair of the American Bar Association's federal judiciary committee, called that "a real revolution." Overall, 15 percent of Carter's appointments to the federal bench were women.

President Reagan has so far appointed more than two hundred judges to the federal bench. "By the end of his second term," according to *The Wall Street Journal*, "he will probably have named more than half of the 743 federal judges in the country." The Reagan appointees may be the longest-lasting legacy of the Reagan administration. Of the total number of judges appointed so far, only forty, or roughly 8 percent, are women.

Women and their supporters are conducting an intense campaign to try to better that percentage. In the judicial branch, as well as in the others, they reason, the presence of women would make a difference.

★ 8 ★

THE PROSPECTS FOR WOMEN

In spite of the growing numbers of women who are now in public office, no one who has watched their progress would say that equality has been achieved. By and large, the country continues to be governed by white, middle-class men, especially at the highest levels. In fact, equal representation for women is an item of unfinished business on democracy's agenda, according to observers such as Bess Myerson, commissioner of the Cultural Affairs Department for New York City. Myerson, herself a political appointee, told a conference of Women in Municipal Government they must keep working to give women a chance.

> Despite the strides women have made, there are too many inequities still around, too many arbitrary obstacles, too many maddening double standards, too many closed doors that should be opened to all who are qualified to enter.
> We need every fine brain, every skilled hand, every voice with something to say.

Winning the vote in 1920 was an empty victory if women have no say in shaping the decisions that impact their lives, Myerson said.

But does it really make a difference when women participate in decision making at the highest levels? Democrat Myerson thinks so. And so does Republican Jeane Kirkpatrick. As the former chief delegate to the United Nations and member of the president's foreign policy team, Kirkpatrick has been in a unique position. She described her experience in a *New York Times* profile by Jane Rosen.

> I was the only woman in our history, I think, who ever sat in regularly at top-level foreign-policy-making meetings. Those arenas have always been closed to women, not only here but in most other countries. And it matters a great deal. It's terribly important, maybe even to the future of the world, for women to take part in making the decisions that shape our destiny.

Kirkpatrick is one of today's women who may get a chance to prove her ideas, according to Rosen. The former ambassador is considered a major political power. She may even have a place on the ballot in the 1988 presidential election.

But what is it that she—or any other woman—might bring to the political process that's different? How is a woman in office different from a man?

MAKING A DIFFERENCE

Ruth Mandel, director of the Center for the American Woman and Politics (CAWP) at Rutgers University, says it's too soon to say conclusively how women will affect the political process. "You're writing science fiction until you have sufficient numbers upon which to base an answer," she says. To show accurately the effect of any population group, including women, in political office, there must be a "critical mass." There are not enough women in office at this time to reach accurate conclusions. But with that understood, there are still some tantalizing clues and trends to observe.

Preliminary research from the Center for the American Woman and Politics shows that women do appear to make a difference. First of all, they have different points of view on critical issues. Women tend to be more liberal on war and peace issues. They are more liberal and progressive on social issues. In fact, conservative women are more liberal than conservative men. And liberal women are more liberal than liberal men.

Women tend to want to put more money into social programs, into education, into welfare for the poor and needy. They tend to want to spend less on the arms race and to put more emphasis on peace efforts. More women support an Equal Rights Amendment. More women support freedom of choice (the right to choose abortion).

In effect, women seem to care more about issues concerned with children, families, and other women's lives. But sensitivity to women's issues does not belong to women only. "There's no way I would attribute new issues—rape, displaced homemakers, etc., to women officeholders alone," Mandel says. These attitudes must be seen as part of a larger movement toward deeper social understanding and support.

As role models, women in office encourage others to follow them on a political path. Women hire women to staff their offices, serving as managers, speechwriters, researchers, and aides. They serve as younger women's mentors, sharing valuable information about how to play the game. They inspire other women to break through the barriers.

In the aftermath of her campaign for vice president, Geraldine Ferraro said, "Without a Bella there could have been no Gerry," referring to former congresswoman and activist Bella Abzug, who always pushed women to strive for their share of power. Following Ferraro's thought, Ruth Mandel says, "Without a Gerry, there could be no Jeane," referring to the range of possibilities that are open to Jeane Kirkpatrick, following Ferraro's trailblazing candidacy.

Susan J. Carroll, author of *Women as Candidates in American Politics*, agrees that conclusions about women in office are premature. Still, she believes that public policy is going to change as more and more women join school boards, city councils, state legislatures, and win seats in the U.S. Congress. Her survey of women candidates shows some differences from their male counterparts.

The thing that surprises me is that women candidates are as strongly feminist as they are. I didn't expect to find attitudinal differences. They *are* more liberal, bringing different perspectives.

Carroll says that women will be placing new issues on the policy agenda. For example, if mass transit is the subject, women are more likely to think about the impact of a bus or train system on an aging parent or on children—rather than thinking only of commuters on their way to work. Carroll says that a broader view of society's needs may develop anyway, but it will happen *faster* because women are there.

> The same would happen if there were more poor people or blacks in office. The experience of being a woman, or minority, and seeing how one's interests are not served is radicalizing.
> Public policy will become more responsive to everyone. But the changes will be in the nuances. There will not necessarily be bold, fundamental changes.

SUPPORT SYSTEMS

As the 1980s roll along, the public is getting used to seeing women in office. But many women want to move the process along more quickly. To achieve this, political education is important. And women's groups—focused wholly on political issues—play a big part in preparing women to be active in public life.

Nonpartisan organizations, such as the National Women's Political Caucus, were founded to promote women in office. The League of Women Voters, which grew out of a woman's suffrage organization, has been educating women in politics for decades. Major political parties have supported women's divisions for a number of years, although it is only recently that they have begun to promote political careers for women rather than just functioning as a support group for men.

But in addition to these organizations, there are other more specialized groups now working to educate women and to get them elected. Many of the groups are organized on a racial or ethnic basis. Among them, Hispanic and black groups are especially active.

Hispanic women, or Latinas, have been urged to make their political presence felt, especially in Texas, the Southwest, and California. Assembly member Gloria Molina was the first Hispanic woman to be elected to the California legislature. Along with Los Angeles deputy mayor Grace Montanez Davis and activist Lucille Roybal, Molina organized the Latina Political Assembly. It was necessary, she said, because "Latinas have been working behind the scenes too long."

According to Molina, Latinas have been active in community affairs throughout history. What's been missing is a mechanism by which they could express their opinions on public policy issues and be recognized as a force. The purpose of the Latina Political Assembly is to ask state and national policymakers to come into the Hispanic community and present their points of view. In turn, these leaders will get feedback from the women and will get to know a vital group of citizens. Both sides benefit from the exchange.

Being connected with a formal structure such as the Latina Political Assembly is the beginning of political visibility for many women. Organizing gives them the opportunity to come together to share ideas and information, to support each other, to create a public presence, and, not least of all, to begin to see each other as possible candidates, and to work together toward such goals.

Working toward these ends, black women have organized themselves into an especially potent political force. In Los Angeles, the thousand-member Black Women's Forum has been flexing its muscles since the beginning of the decade. Assembly member Maxine Waters, who helped organize the forum, says that membership in such an organization can be a real advantage. She told *Black Enterprise* writer Pamela Douglas that being connected gives her clout.

I understand the strength of alliance with women's groups throughout California. So my male colleagues view me differently. They're not dealing with an isolated woman. I can affect their votes. I have purposely developed this leverage. When bills are proposed, they consult me because I'm plugged into a statewide network.

Ironically, when Waters first ran for office, the Speaker of the California Assembly said, "Maxine Waters is a nice lady, but she ain't gonna win." Given her impressive support network, no one would say that about her today.

MONEY AND PACs

If a political candidate can bring in plenty of volunteers, that's good. If she can get the endorsement of her political party and of various groups, that's good. But if she can raise lots of money, that's very good.

Money buys radio and TV advertising. It pays for brochures and flyers. It pays for polls and expert advice. It makes possible campaign headquarters, office equipment, and professional campaign workers. But without funds to buy such goods and services, only the most extraordinary candidate can win in a competitive election.

Linda Hallenborg, who has raised thousands of dollars for the National Women's Political Caucus, says that money is the crucial factor in women's campaigns. Because female candidates are often in the position of challenging incumbent males, they have to work much harder than their opponents for recognition and credibility. In order to get the voters' attention, they need money and they need it early in the game, Hallenborg says.

> If we're going to have a truly national movement of women in political office, the only way we're going to achieve our goals is to organize and to raise money and to provide the *early money* for women candidates. Early money will allow women to get into the race, to do polling to provide themselves with the material which will enable them to win the election.
>
> Without the money—which will almost invariably come from the women PACs—they don't stand a chance of winning.

At this point in history, women's political action committees (PACs) are helping many women become viable candidates. Men have long benefited from campaign donations made by

These members of the National Women's Political Caucus are attending an issue briefing on Capitol Hill, one of the events sponsored by the organization that promotes women as candidates for public office.

major groups such as the Democratic and Republican parties, professional organizations, and lobbies such as the National Rifle Association and the National Association of Realtors. But these groups tend to give money to people with whom they are already associated or to people who are already in office. Women are frequently passed over when campaign funds are distributed. Because of this, PACs have been created which are devoted primarily to women.

The biggest and most visible of these PACs are based in Washington, D.C. These include party-affiliated groups such as the Eleanor Roosevelt Fund of the Democratic National Committee, the Campaign Fund for Republican Women, and the fledgling GOP Women's Political Action League. Bipartisan groups are the Women's Campaign Fund and the PACs attached to the National Organization for Women (NOW) and the National Women's Political Caucus (NWPC).

These organizations channel money primarily to candidates in congressional and statewide races. On the local level, individual chapters of NOW and NWPC raise money for city, county, and state candidates. There are also increasing numbers of special local groups such as the Committee of 21 in New Orleans and the Women's Issues Network PAC of Connecticut. Of all the PACs, NOW has been the most successful in raising money, having passed the million-dollar mark in the 1984 elections.

Guidelines for giving money to female candidates vary. Some groups insist their candidates pass muster on a questionnaire that surveys their attitudes and positions. Only those women who see eye to eye with the group get money. On the other hand, some partisan organizations will give campaign funds to any woman who looks like she can win her race— provided that she meets some simple basic criteria such as Republican or Democratic party memberships.

Most women's PACs lean toward liberal or progressive candidates, especially on women's issues. There is presently no ultraconservative PAC for women candidates. Conservative political groups provide funds for both male and female candidates who meet their approval.

Most women's PACs now in operation are in the process of learning how to raise money. Asking individuals and businesses to pull out their checkbooks in behalf of a candidate is an art that must be practiced to be successful. Many women have been traditionally shy about asking for money, except for causes that everyone can agree on, such as charities or civic improvement funds. Female candidates and their backers have to learn to say, "I'm the best person for this job and I want your support."

Regionally, the most successful fund raisers are a discreet but powerful corps of women in Texas. This group, which does not broadcast its name, can raise hundreds of thousands of dollars overnight. They believe that any woman who is really trying can raise $10,000 within six months. When Ann Richards was deciding whether to run for state treasurer, the Texas women raised $350,000 literally overnight, making Richards a viable contender.

On the other hand, there are groups such as the Hawaii Women's Political Action League, which operates more like a volunteer club. Through coffees, bake sales, and such, they raise money dollar by dollar. Their object is to learn the fundamentals of politics without being overwhelmed. In this case, the PAC functions like a running political seminar. Honolulu City Council president Patsy Mink told *Women's PACs* author Katherine Kleeman that the group is grooming its members as well as aiding candidates.

> We'll have a lot of competent women who'll be able to hold themselves out not only as candidates, but as managers, treasurers, counselors, advisors, strategists—a pool of people who have been in an active role as we have never had in the history of politics.

Most PAC groups, however, are less active than the Hawaii group and much less affluent than the Texas group. To date, few PACs have raised as much as $100,000 in any one election year, according to Kleeman.

To collect money, the average PAC relies on a list of sponsors who give $100 or more each election season. Money comes from a variety of fund-raising efforts such as auctioning off donated artwork and merchandise, holding public programs with guest speakers, sponsoring concerts, dances, picnics, and other social events. The aim is to capture money from their own membership, as well as from the general public and targeted donors.

According to Kleeman's report for the Center for the American Woman and Politics, the membership in most PACs is middle- to upper-class white women. Many are professionals—lawyers, teachers, nurses, journalists, etc. The candidate questionnaires that many of these PACs use are a tool for rating "feminist" and "progressive" views.

In the case of the Hawaii Women's Political Action League, women who want to be endorsed have to fill out a two-page policy statement that covers a wide variety of issues. World peace, the ERA, child care, economic policies, health care, sex exploitation, community services, education, and work philosophy are among the items on which the prospective candidate must rate herself.

The East Bay Women's Political Action Committee of Berkeley, California, has been even more specific. This group insisted that its candidates support a five-point program:

—women's health/reproductive freedom;
—educational equality for women;
—economic justice for women;
—protection of women in home/workplace;
—protection of environment and quality of life

In addition to the hundreds or thousands of dollars a candidate may be awarded by a PAC, she herself must also raise money from other sources. Whether the candidate likes it or not, she'll have to learn to ask for it. According to Marcia Kelley, Salem, Oregon, campaign manager, women simply have to plunge in.

Here in Salem, a House race costs about $35,000. To earn that kind of money, the candidate has to be in touch with a wide variety of people. Starting with her Christmas card list, she has to go to everyone she has known since college. From that she branches out to peripheral acquaintances, then on to the membership lists of every organization she's ever belonged to.

Kelley says the water isn't so bad once the candidate plunges. In most cases people are glad to contribute. They only have to be asked.

Campaign schools are also available to teach women how to raise money. The Republicans, for instance, tutor women candidates in budgeting, polling, research, issue development, and headquarters management. But it's in fund raising that women need the most help. Campaign teacher Sallie Barre says that women need to learn strategies. She told *The Saturday Evening Post* that women may ask for money but then they fail to make sure it's delivered.

> That's where we fall down. Women don't know how to close a deal. They know how to put on a party, but they don't know how to say, "Do you want to write me a check now or put it on your VISA card?" The words stick in their throats. We show them how to overcome that.

GETTING TOUGH

One of the chief lessons women have learned in American politics is that losing does not mean defeat. Each campaign for office teaches something; each failure to win a position or to get a bill through the city council or the legislature shows something about how to win the next time around. On the campaign trail and in office, women are getting tougher and wiser.

For example, in 1980 in Illinois, State Representative Carol Moseley Braun believed a voter redistricting plan was unfair. Braun, who represented a black and Hispanic district on Chicago's South Side, thought the new plan weakened minority representation. Ignoring the fury of other Democrats who favored the plan, Braun sued the party over the new boundaries. If she had lost the suit, her political career would likely have ended.

"I guess they didn't think I had the chutzpah to sue," she commented. But she won, and the dispute was largely forgotten. In 1985, Braun was elevated to serve as assistant House majority leader.

In Vermont, Republican Susan Auld won good committee assignments for Republican women by challenging the House Speaker. In Toledo, Ohio, Mayor Donna Owens stepped into the middle of a bitter dispute between a leading union and a manufacturer. She cooled their tempers and found a solution.

Most women's political leaders believe that today's female public officials are building a solid foundation for the future. They believe that gender will be no barrier to office up to and including the presidency. Kathy Wilson, immediate past chair of the National Women's Political Caucus, says that a tide is flowing that cannot be stopped. At the 1985 convention of NWPC, she reaffirmed the goals that established the group in 1971.

> We in the Caucus are undeterred by the results of any given election cycle and undaunted by the fashionable political posture of the day. Persistence, you might say, is our middle name. There are some political analysts who don't understand this about us. They don't understand that being discouraged every now and then is not synonymous with being defeated. They don't understand the depth of our commitment to women's rights and the extent of our staying power. They also don't understand the very special nature of our function within the American political process.
>
> We in the Caucus are in the business, not only of winning elections, but of winning hearts and minds. We know that candidates come and go. We know that administrations change. But once the mind makes a change . . . once it comes to accept the concept of equality for all people . . . once the heart truly believes that women and men should coexist as partners . . . then, my sisters, it is at that very moment that our victory has been won.

PREPARING FOR THE FUTURE

Most of the women who run PACs, who work in the various women's political caucuses, and who attend workshops to sharpen their capabilities and to find support for future goals are already somewhat experienced in politics. They are part of the savvy network of women getting older and wiser in the political system. But where should a young woman go who is interested in a career in politics?

CAWP director Ruth Mandel says that a young woman can gain a lot from being a volunteer, rubbing elbows with her seniors. Age makes no difference when it comes to working for the public interest.

> Get involved in the community. Find a campaign or issue that you're interested in. You're really needed in most circles, and you don't have to be an expert. You don't have to be fifty years old. If you show that you care and you're consistent, there is tremendous mobility to be promoted at a very early age.

Mandel says a young woman need not go to Washington, D.C., to get a first-class education in politics. What's needed is people who are broadly educated—who know the liberal arts and sciences. There is no such thing as a degree in "politician."

When she ran for vice president, Geraldine Ferraro showed the nation a woman who could be courageous, direct, and sharp without losing the warmth of her personality or her sense of humor. Americans got a good look at female charisma in politics. Ferraro made history. The future will build on that history, says writer Susan Bolotin. She predicts a new woman in politics.

> The actions of today's strong and determined political women will create new ideals, new myths based not on men who ride high in the saddle but on women who have led honorable and courageous lives.
>
> It will be up to tomorrow's women to personify these myths, to be the charismatic leaders of our country.

FOR FURTHER READING

Abzug, Bella, with Mim Kelber. *Gender Gap: Bella Abzug's Guide to Political Power for American Women*. Boston: Houghton Mifflin, 1984. (A former three-term member of Congress offers a liberal feminist perspective on American politics.)

Ferraro, Geraldine A., with Linda Bird Francke. *My Story*. New York: Bantam Books, 1985. (Ferraro describes her experience as the first woman candidate for vice president.)

Flexner, Eleanor. *Century of Struggle: The Woman's Rights Movement in the United States*. New York: Atheneum, 1973. (An engrossing account of the woman's rights movement in the United States.)

Gluck, Sherna, ed. *From Parlor to Prison: Five American Suffragists Talk about Their Lives*. New York: Vintage Books, 1976. (Fascinating first-person perspectives on the struggle for woman suffrage.)

Gurko, Miriam. *The Ladies of Seneca Falls: the Birth of the Woman's Rights Movement*. New York: Macmillan, 1974. (An account of the feminist movements of the eighteenth and nineteenth centuries, focusing on Elizabeth Cady Stanton and Susan B. Anthony.)

Josephson, Hannah. *Jeannette Rankin, First Lady in Congress.* Indianapolis: Bobbs-Merrill, 1974. (A biography of a trailblazer whose life mirrors the woman's rights movement in the twentieth century.)

McHenry, Robert, ed. *Famous American Women: A Biographical Dictionary from Colonial Times to the Present.* New York: Dove, 1980. (A useful resource for research and reports on women in politics.)

Mandel, Ruth B. *In the Running: The New Woman Candidate.* Boston: Beacon Press, 1983.

Trafton, Barbara M. *Women Winning: How to Run for Office.* Boston: The Harvard Common Press, 1984.

Booklets available from Center for the American Woman and Politics, Eagleton Institute of Politics, Rutgers—The State University of New Jersey, New Brunswick, NY 08901: *Women's Routes to Elective Office*, by Susan J. Carroll and Wendy S. Strimling; *Political Women Tell What it Takes*, by Kathy A. Stanwick; *Women Make a Difference*, by Kathy A. Stanwick and Katherine E. Kleeman. All published in 1983.

INDEX